PENGUIN CLASSICS

THE PRINCE

NICCOLÒ MACHIAVELLI was born in Florence in 1469 of an old citizen family. Little is known about his life until 1498, when he was appointed secretary and Second Chancellor to the Florentine Republic. During his time of office his journeys included missions to Louis XII and to the Emperor Maximilian; he was with Cesare Borgia in the Romagna; and after watching the Papal election of 1503 he accompanied Julius II on his first campaign of conquest. In 1507, as chancellor of the newly appointed *Nove di Milizia*, he organized an infantry force which fought at the capture of Pisa in 1509. Three years later it was defeated by the Holy League at Prato, the Medici returned to Florence, and Machiavelli was excluded from public life. After suffering imprisonment and torture, he retired to his farm near San Casciano, where he lived with his wife and six children and gave his time to study and writing. His works included *The Prince*; the *Discourses on the First Decade of Livy*; *The Art of War*; and the comedy, *Mandragola*, a satire on seduction. In 1520, Cardinal Giulio de' Medici secured him a commission to write a history of Florence, which he finished in 1525. After a brief return to public life, he died in 1527.

GEORGE BULL is an author and journalist who has translated six volumes for Penguin Classics: Benvenuto Cellini's *Autobiography*, *The Book of the Courtier* by Castiglione, Vasari's *Lives of the Artists* (two volumes), *The Prince* by Machiavelli and Pietro Aretino's *Selected Letters*. After reading History at Brasenose College, Oxford, George Bull worked for the *Financial Times*, McGraw-Hill *World News*, and for the *Director* magazine, of which he was Editor-in-Chief until 1984. He was appointed Director of the Anglo-Japanese Economic Institute in 1986. He is a director of Central Banking Publications and the founder and publisher of the quarterly publications *Insight Japan* and *International Minds*. His books include *Vatican Politics*; *Bid for Power* (with Anthony Vice), a history of take-over bids; *Renaissance Italy*, a book for children; *Venice: The Most Triumphant City*; *Inside the Vatican*; a translation from the Italian of *The Pilgrim: The Travels of Pietro della Valle*; and *Michelangelo: A Biography*

(Penguin, 1996; St Martin's Press N.Y., 1997). George Bull was elected a Fellow of the Royal Society of Literature in 1981 and a Vice-President of the British-Italian Society in 1994. He was awarded an OBE in the 1990 New Year's Honours List.

ANTHONY GRAFTON teaches European intellectual history at Princeton University. He is the author of *Joseph Scaliger: A Study in the History of Classical Scholarship*, *Defenders of the Text* and *The Footnote: A Curious History*.

NICCOLÒ MACHIAVELLI

The Prince

Translated with Notes by
GEORGE BULL
With an Introduction by
ANTHONY GRAFTON

PENGUIN BOOKS

PENGUIN BOOKS

Published by the Penguin Group
Penguin Books Ltd, 27 Wrights Lane, London w8 5tz, England
Penguin Putnam Inc., 375 Hudson Street, New York, New York 10014, USA
Penguin Books Australia Ltd, Ringwood, Victoria, Australia
Penguin Books Canada Ltd, 10 Alcorn Avenue, Toronto, Ontario, Canada m4v 3b2
Penguin Books (NZ) Ltd, Private Bag 102902, NSMC, Auckland, New Zealand

Penguin Books Ltd, Registered Offices: Harmondsworth, Middlesex, England

First published 1961
Reprinted with corrections 1975
Reprinted with corrections 1981
Reprinted with corrections 1995
New edition 1999
3 5 7 9 10 8 6 4

Copyright © George Bull, 1961, 1975, 1981, 1995, 1999
Introduction copyright © Anthony Grafton, 1999
All rights reserved

Set in 10/13 pt PostScript Monotype Bembo
Typeset by Rowland Phototypesetting Ltd, Bury St Edmunds, Suffolk
Printed in England by Clays Ltd, St Ives plc

For my wife

CONTENTS

CHRONOLOGY

1469 MAY: Birth in Florence of Niccolò di Bernardo Machiavelli (M) to Bernardo and Bartolomea (née de' Nelli).

1475 Sixtus IV (della Rovere) elected Pope.

1481 With his brother Totto, M begins to attend the school of Paolo da Ronciglione.

1484 Innocent VIII (Cibo) elected Pope.

late 1480s M attends lectures by Marcello Virgilio Adriani.

1491 Savonarola as preacher begins to win influence in Florence.

1492 APRIL: Death of Lorenzo de' Medici. Piero becomes head of the family. Alexander VI (Borgia) elected Pope.

1494 NOV: Piero and the Medici are expelled from Florence. French troops enter the city.

1498 MAY: Savonarola executed for heresy.

JUNE: M is confirmed by the Great Council as second chancellor of the Republic.

JULY: M elected secretary to the Ten of War.

NOV: M is sent on his first diplomatic mission to Piombino on behalf of the Ten of War.

1499 Mission to Caterina Sforza-Riario, ruler of Imola and Forli.

1500 JULY: Six-month mission to King Louis XII of France.

1501 M marries Marietta Corsini. (They will have six children.)

1502 Piero Soderini elected *gonfaloniere* for life.

OCT: M begins mission to the court of Cesare Borgia (Duke Valentino) at Imola.

DEC: M follows Cesare to Cesena and Senigallia.

1503 For M's plan to assert Florentine authority over Pisa (in revolt against Florence from 1502–9), Leonardo da Vinci is consulted on a scheme to divert the river Arno around Pisa to the sea at Livorno.

APRIL: M sent on mission to Pandolfo Petrucci, ruler of Siena.

SEPT: Election of Pope Pius III (Piccolimini).

OCT: M sent on mission to Papal Court at Rome.

NOV: Election of Pope Julius II (della Rovere).

1504 JAN: M's second mission to court of King Louis XII.

JULY: M's second mission to Pandolfo Petrucci.

1505 DEC: M becomes secretary to the new committee, the Nine of the Militia.

1506 JAN: M recruits for the militia in the Mugello, north of Florence.

AUG–OCT: M's second mission to the Papal Court follows Pope Julius from Viterbo to Orvieto, Perugia, Urbino, Cesena, and Imola.

1507 DEC: M sent on mission to court of the Emperor Maximilian.

1510 JUNE–SEPT: M's third mission to the court of King Louis XII.

1511 SEPT: M's fourth mission to the court of King Louis XII.

1512 After Spanish troops invade Florentine territory – and sack Prato – Florence surrenders, Soderini is deposed and goes into exile as the Medici return to power.

NOV: M is dismissed from the Chancery and sentenced to a year's confinement within Florentine territory.

1513 FEB: M is tried for conspiracy, tortured, and imprisoned.

MARCH–APRIL: After his release M retires to his farm at Sant' Andrea in Percussina, seven miles south of Florence.

MARCH: Election of Pope Leo X (Giovanni de' Medici).

JULY: M drafts *The Prince* (*Il Principe*).

1515 M joins a discussion group – interested in politics and literature – meeting at Orti Oricellari, Florence. He begins to write the *Discourses* (*Discorsi*), dedicating his commentary on the first ten books of Livy's *History of Rome* to Zanobi Buondelmonti and Cosimo Rucellai, grandson of Bernardo Rucellai who had laid out the Oricellari gardens.

c. 1516 Manuscript copies of *The Prince* begin to circulate in and beyond Florence.

1518 M writes his ribald play *The Mandrake Root* (*Mandragola*) and about now finishes the *Discourses*.

1520 M writes the book on military organization, *Art of War* (*Arte della Guerra*) and *Life of Castruccio Castracani of Lucca* (*La vita di Castruccio Castracani da Lucca*), as well as a *Summary* of Lucca's system of government. He is commissioned to write the history of Florence by Cardinal Giulio de' Medici.

1521 *Art of War* is published.

1522 Cardinal Adrian Florensz is elected Pope as Adrian VI.

1523 Cardinal Giulio de' Medici is elected Pope as Clement VII.

1525 M visits Rome to present his finished *History of Florence* (*Istorie Fiorentine*) to Pope Clement. M's *Mandragola* is performed and acclaimed in Venice, which he later visits on a mission to settle a trade dispute for the Wool Guild of Florence.

1526 M revises his play, *Mandragola*.

1527 MAY: The city of Rome is brutally sacked by the Imperialist Army of chiefly Germans and Spaniards under the Duke of Bourbon. The Medici are expelled from Florence where the Republic adopts a new constitution.

21 JUNE: M dies and is buried in the church of Santa Croce.

1531/32 Posthumous publication of the *Discourses*, *The Prince* and the *History of Florence*.

Italy in 1500

INTRODUCTION

The tyrant terrifies his subjects. Spying balefully on the world from his strongly fortified palace, as sensitive to approaching prey or predators as a spider delicately balanced at the centre of a web, he dominates the life of all around him. He takes credit for the achievements of nobler men who spend their substance on civic projects, like great churches and other fine buildings. Entertaining the ambassadors of foreign powers at his own table, he makes decisions that affect the well-being of all of his subjects without consulting anyone except his favourites. He turns his entire state into a machine for his own profit and that of a few friends. And he does not shrink from robbing wealthy men of their possessions or pure young women of their virtue. All threats to his sole authority he resists with absolute ferocity.

This description of a prince – solitary, vicious, grindingly cruel to those who stand in his way – sounds at first like a stray page from Machiavelli's *Prince*, a book which teaches effective tactics for the absolute ruler, and which many readers have seen as preaching ruthlessness and even glorying in bloodshed. But it comes from a very different source: the *Treatise on the Government of Florence* of the Dominican friar Girolamo Savonarola, whose years of domination in Florentine politics, from 1494 to 1498, coincided with the beginning of Machiavelli's mature life. The parallels between these two very different men are striking. Like Machiavelli, Savonarola led an active civic life, trying to preserve the republican form of government, which he saw as ideal for Florence, and wrote intense, powerfully imagined treatises on politics. Like Machiavelli, Savonarola cherished classical ideals: he believed that the Romans had created, if not a perfect, at least an exemplary republic – one whose institutions formed its citizens to be virtuous, by making them participate regularly in civic life. Like Machiavelli, Savonarola experienced political realities at their most brutal. He knew the tactics and psychologies of Italy's tyrants, as well as the local traditions of the Florentine republic, as his portrait of the tyrannical ruler shows. Worse still, he knew what it meant to lose the support of those who meant most to him. When his challenge to the authority of the Roman popes brought the interdict on his fellow Florentines, endangering their property and commercial ventures, many turned against him. One prominent citizen remarked, in an emergency meeting, that Savonarola deserved support but could not have it, since 'we in Italy are as we are'. Property mattered more than loyalty – a proposition Machiavelli actually repeated in *The Prince*, when he remarked that men could forget the loss of their fathers more rapidly than that of their property. Like Machiavelli, finally, Savonarola saw his political career come to a disastrous end. The author of *The Prince* suffered political ostracism, the Dominican preacher underwent public execution in the Piazza della Signoria and became, for Machiavelli, the prototype of the unarmed prophet whose career, in the real world, must end in disaster.[1]

Machiavelli's *Prince* reads, when one comes to it without knowledge of its context, like an abstract manual, one whose tenets apply almost as well to a modern corporation as to a Renaissance state. But as the case of Savonarola suggests, Machiavelli was in many ways a characteristic product of Florence, the city in which he came to maturity, in whose government he served from 1498 to 1512, and for which he wrote the series of dazzlingly original books for which he is chiefly remembered: notably *The Prince*, the *Discourses on the First Decade of Livy*, the *History of Florence* and *Mandragola*. Machiavelli's obsessive interest in how politics work, his passion for gossip about important men and high affairs, his desperate effort to frame rules that could predict how men would respond to political challenges and crises – all these and many other traits of character and intellect were shared with a large number of his fellow citizens. So were the political experiences that led him to depart from normal Florentine beliefs on some vital points. In both form and content *The Prince* owes an enormous amount to the peculiar society and culture in which its author grew up, worked, thought and met his own political crisis.

The Florence Machiavelli knew and served was one of the two great republics that still flourished, in the later years of the fifteenth century, among the larger states, above all Milan, the Papal states and Naples, that were coming to dominate the Italian peninsula. One of the largest cities in Europe, it had suffered badly during the plague years of the fourteenth century, and the Florentine cloth industry – the backbone of the city's medieval expansion – contracted alongside the European population which had bought its products. In the course of the fifteenth century, however, the city returned to prosperity on both the private and the public level, even if it no longer matched the independent power of the other great republic, Venice. Florentine bankers and traders continued to amass vast fortunes; the new silk industry supplied some of the income lost by the decline in the wool business. Florence became the centre of a territorial state, one which included previously independent cities like Pisa and Livorno. It developed a wide range of new institutions to cope with the practical problems that developed, from a new system of taxation based on property, the *catasto*, to a galley fleet based in Pisa.

The city became one of the centres of the new classical culture purveyed by the humanists of the Renaissance: the teachers and intellectuals who fostered schools and libraries for the study of the Greek and Latin classics. In other cities, like Milan, such studies depended on princely patronage. In Florence, by contrast, they were closely linked with the urban élite and the local civic government. Florence had the first great public secular library of modern times, that of San Marco, founded by a patrician book-collector and connoisseur, Niccolò Niccoli. From the last years of the fourteenth century, the city's chancellors – the high officials who wrote official correspondence and propaganda – from Coluccio Salutati onwards, supported the study of the classics. They and the young intellectuals they worked with, like Leonardo Bruni, used the evidence of Roman history to insist that Florence itself was a direct and worthy descendant of republican Rome, and drew on the political thought of Cicero and Aristotle to argue for the superior quality of the active life led by Florentine citizens. In other words, long before Machiavelli's lifetime the city had become a centre of the new, classical style in education and scholarship. By the middle of the fifteenth century, patricians as well as civil servants regularly cited classical examples in the course of public debates to justify modern policy choices. Even the setting for political discussion became more classical. The artistic revolution of the fifteenth century, which began in Florence, radically altered the city's physiognomy, as private families began to consolidate large city landholdings on which they built severe, enormous palaces, with rusticated façades and colonnaded court-yards. In place of the old merchant houses, their ground-floor shops open to the street, rose enormous classical structures, closed and monumental.[2]

Even those Florentine discussions of politics that were most aus-terely classical in style dealt with extremely practical questions. In the course of the fifteenth century, the city survived a series of long, debilitating wars; with Giangaleazzo Visconti of Milan, Ladislas of Naples and others. The strains these imposed, in turn, gradually became too great for the city's republican form of government to bear. In 1433–4 Cosimo de' Medici, who had been exiled from Florence by his opponents, returned to the city. He did not overturn the republic but transformed it by subtle manipulation, taking control of the procedures used to select members of the city's governing committees by lot. Cosimo insisted that he was only a Florentine citizen, and even his panegyrists called him only *pater patriae*, despite the range of his power and the vast scale of his building programmes making his status in the city obvious.

In the next two generations, the Medici emerged as the clear rulers of the city, even though the old institutions of the republic survived. Cosimo's grandson, Lorenzo the Magnificent, left few open questions about the extent of his powers. Resident ambassadors from other powers actually lived with him in the Medici palace, and he personally negotiated his way out of the most serious public crises that confronted him, like the war waged against Florence in 1478 by Pope Sixtus IV and King Ferrante of Naples, after the members of another great family, the Pazzi, failed in an attempt to assassinate Lorenzo. In the sixteenth century, when foreign powers ravaged Italy and the independence of the fifteenth century was permanently lost, men looked back to the era of Lorenzo as a golden age, in which his diplomatic skills had held the contending powers of Italy in balance, while his patronage and support had encouraged brilliant artists like Botticelli and writers like Poliziano. Lorenzo himself wrote sonnets and carnival songs, including the famous, haunting *Quant'è bella giovinezza*.[3]

In 1494 the French King Charles VIII invaded Italy. Lorenzo had died in 1492. Lorenzo's son Piero, no match for his father at dealing with either domestic or foreign threats, alienated many influential citizens before the crisis came. When the French appeared, he capitulated without a fight. On his return to Florence, he found that much of the city had risen against him. At this critical moment, Savonarola came to the fore. He had long denounced his fellow Italians for their vices, and predicted the imminent coming of disaster. When Charles VIII materialized on cue, Savonarola won enormous prestige, not only for predicting the French deluge, but also for convincing Charles, as many believed, to spare the city.

Drawing on Florentine prophetic traditions which had circulated for centuries, Savonarola began to predict that the city would play a great, creative role in the coming reformation of the church. He also insisted that the Florentines, given their political energy and passion, could live only in a republic, and staked his prestige on the creation of a new form of government, centred on a Great Council, in which a large number of citizens would participate. This institution came into being, along with a hall for its meetings, which Leonardo and Michelangelo were assigned to decorate. Florence entered into a last, protracted experiment with republicanism, one that would last, despite the crisis of 1498 and Savonarola's own downfall, until 1512.[4]

Piero Soderini, the *gonfaloniere*, came to dominate this republic, desperately trying to reconcile the great patricians and tradesmen who saw their interests as radically different. And Machiavelli – who entered the service of the Ten of War in 1498 – spent his entire political career in the service of Soderini's government. He became an accomplished civil servant, expert in governmental procedures and fluent in both interpreting and producing official correspondence. He served both on missions within the Florentine state and as a diplomat abroad. Working sometimes in collaboration with Francesco Vettori, a close friend of higher birth, he came to know the most powerful rulers of his time, in Italy and the north alike: Cesare Borgia, Louis XII of France, the Holy Roman Emperor Maximilian I. Sometimes humiliated by the representatives of greater powers, he came to see how little Florence counted for in the new politics and warfare of the early sixteenth century. Eternally curious, he also came to see how Florence and other large states were going about the business of making themselves more powerful, and made himself into an articulate, pungent critic of Florentine policies, one whose memoranda, in the tradition of the Florentine chancery, often bristled with examples from Roman history, carefully chosen to shed light on the present. Convinced that only a citizen army would fight loyally to the end, Machiavelli, working for a new committee, the Nine, actually created a militia to defend Florence, only to see it swept away in a day by the soldiers who destroyed the Soderini regime and restored the Medici to power in 1512.[5] Coming under suspicion of conspiracy against the returned Medici, Machiavelli, after being arrested and tortured, retired from the city to his small farm in the country, a few miles away, where he tormented himself anew with his desire to return to the metropolis and to politics. Machiavelli's political life, in other words, began and ended in invasion and revolution. No wonder that he saw the political order as so fragile, and insisted that its preservation must take precedence over the scruples of tender, traditionalist minds.

These were the circumstances in which Machiavelli wrote letter after letter to Vettori, debating the political interpretation of recent events and, as Vettori insisted on the inscrutability of princes, insisting in his own turn that he had mastered the art of reading princely actions and intentions.[6] Driven to despair by his exclusion from the world of politics, and clinging to the hope that his political skills might win him back the position of power he had lost, Machiavelli turned to the classical culture and political experience of his native city in the confidence that he could find in them the intellectual resources he needed. In the most famous of these letters, he described at length how he found himself forced to live, confined to village gossip, fishing and gambling, reading one of the newly fashionable pocket editions of the love poets, arguing with his poor, silly neighbours. And he tried to turn tragedy into triumph by showing that he could transcend these troubles by exercising his skills as analyst of past and present:

When evening comes, I return to my home, and I go into my study; and on the threshold, I take off my everyday clothes, which are covered with mud and mire, and I put on regal and curial robes; and dressed in a more appropriate manner I enter into the ancient courts of ancient men and am welcomed by them kindly, and there I taste the food that alone is mine, and for which I was born; and there I am not ashamed to speak to them, to ask them the reasons for their actions; and they, in their humanity, answer me; and for four hours I feel no boredom, I dismiss every affliction, I no longer fear poverty nor do I tremble at the thought of death: I become completely part of them. And as Dante says that knowledge does not exist without the retention of it by memory, I have noted down what I have learned from their conversation, and I composed a little book, *De principatibus*, where I delve as deeply as I can into thoughts on this subject, discussing what a principality is, what kinds there are, how they are acquired, how they are maintained, why they are lost.[7]

Machiavelli turned to the traditional resource of the scholar – reading the classics – not only for diversion but in desperation. He hoped that by doing so he could not only understand his own situation, but prove his supreme expertise, and by doing so win a position with the new government of the Medici, one in which his talents would not rust in rural isolation. Accordingly, he dedicated his work to Giuliano de' Medici, in the hope that his thoughts might prove welcome to 'a new prince'. In other words, Machiavelli relied on the resources of the humanistic tradition – knowledge of the classics and eloquence in expression – to win him back a position in which he could lead the active political life he craved more than anything else.

At first glance the book Machiavelli wrote to demonstrate his prowess as a political analyst looks as traditional as his methods. Many humanists before him, from Petrarch onwards, had addressed the topic of the ideal prince. Like Machiavelli, they had discussed the way in which such a prince should be educated, the moral and intellectual qualities he needed most, and how he should deal with his subjects. Their works were crammed, like Machiavelli's, with classical examples of good and bad conduct, which they drew from ancient biographers and historians. The chapter titles of *The Prince* – which Machiavelli wrote in Latin, rather than the Italian in which he wrote the text, and which proposed for discussion such traditional topics as whether a prince should wish for love or fear from his subjects – offered clear signposts to any well-read person: Machiavelli and his readers would tread a path on which many others had gone before them.

Yet from the first, Machiavelli insisted on the originality of his approach to even the most traditional of the questions he addressed. Earlier humanist treatises on the ideal prince began with general ethical principles – the nature of man, the purpose of government, the connection of both to the pursuit of the virtuous life. Machiavelli. By contrast, he boldly claimed, that he would treat politics as it really is. He divided all principalities into two categories, new and established, and he explained, without making any value judgements, what a prince would need to do in each case in order to hold on to his kingdom.

Earlier treatises assumed that a prince needed above all to be good: to pursue virtue, in the traditional sense. Writers like Bartolomeo Platina and Francesco Patrizi offered, in essence, long lists of the virtues that a prince should cultivate and the vices he should avoid, each supported with ample anecdotes from classical sources. Their treatments reflected contemporary realities: humanist writers recognized that kings sought fame in this world, as well as eternal life in the next, praised them for liberal support of culture and learning rather than for parsimony, and sometimes showed considerable psychological shrewdness. Machiavelli also spoke of virtue, constantly. But he used the term 'virtue' in many senses, including that of the basic ability needed, independent of any questions about good or evil, to keep control of one's subjects and one's kingdoms. Accordingly, Machiavelli often told the reader that qualities traditionally considered as 'virtuous', in the Christian or feudal senses, were not virtuous at all in a prince. Liberality, for example, was one of the best-established of princely virtues. Yet if pursued seriously, it must lead to lavishness, to ostentation, to the wasting of the prince's substance and the oppression of his subjects, and, in the end, to the prince's being despised and hated by them. A prince who truly understood 'virtue' – in the sense of the qualities needed to perpetuate his state and his own power – would prefer the 'vice' of meanness to the 'virtue' of liberality. Again and again, Machiavelli transformed the values traditionally highlighted and praised in formal writings on political theory.[8]

Machiavelli himself directed the reader's attention to the radical differences between his approach and that of his predecessors. Others, he wrote in Chapter 15, had discussed republics that did not exist anywhere on earth. He, by contrast, would discuss 'the effective reality of things' – states, rulers and subjects as they really were. He would not offer rules for good behaviour in, for example, the Christian sense. More than once he insisted that a truly Christian prince who kept faith, while other princes did not, or sought his subjects' love rather than trying to make them fear him, would inevitably lose his position. Cicero insisted in *De officiis*, a work continually quoted and applauded by the humanists, that a virtuous man should gain his ends by communication and persuasion rather than by force or treachery, the tactics appropriate to animals – the lion and the fox, respectively. Machiavelli, by contrast, argued that the prince must sometimes act the powerful, decisive lion, sometimes the wily, elusive fox. By doing so he underlined his conviction that the prince could not be constrained by the demands of normal morality if he hoped to do his job properly.[9] Machiavelli, in short, confronted his reader from the start with his realization that straightforward efforts to master and apply the tenets of traditional morality would not produce an effective ruler. Politics must have its own rules.

Machiavelli made these radical innovations in political theory, as Felix Gilbert has shown,[10] to a considerable extent simply by transferring the accumulated Florentine experience of politics from the private sphere of governmental discussions of policy to the public one of political writing. The Florentine government had for a long time convoked meetings of the most influential citizens every time that the state faced a major crisis, and the participants of these invoked classical and modern precedents as regularly and realistically as Machiavelli himself. They tried to formulate rules that would help them understand both the changes in the larger political sphere, as great powers warred over the Italian peninsula, and the upheavals in their own Florentine world, as continual revolutions racked their beloved city. And they framed these in terms as sharp and biting as the most rigorous of Machiavelli's own formulations. Threatened by a foreign power, Florentines might say, 'Dogs that bark don't bite.' More generally, Florentine patricians knew that political actions depended for their success not on divine aid but on the extent of one's skill and the resources with which one computed the possibilities. In 1496, when Florence was endangered by its policy of loyalty to France, one leading citizen remarked that Florence could 'resist either with force or with intelligence. And it does not appear possible that we can resist the whole of Italy relying on force. We must take the alternative: intelligence.' Long before *The Prince* could reach the bookstands of Renaissance princes who might scan its pages eagerly for the secrets of effective political action, the patricians of Florence had discussed politics in a fully realistic way, appreciating that the diverse interests of states and individuals, rather than the ideas they cited, drove their actions. From the 1490s onwards, moreover, the experience of dealing with impetuous rulers like Cesare Borgia and the great armies of the French made Florentines more and more aware that force seemed to rule human affairs. Earlier patricians had praised the policy of delay and urged compromise. By the time Machiavelli wrote *The Prince*, he was only one of many Florentine 'prophets of force'.[11] Both the concepts and the images that Machiavelli used to describe the successful prince, in other words, came to a considerable extent from the political language of the Florentine élite.

No chapter of *The Prince* is more famous, for example, than that in which Machiavelli tried to assess the extent of human freedom of action. There, as elsewhere, he argued that fortune had enormous powers over men. Sometimes, like the river Arno, it swept everything away before it, destroying – as the French invasion had – all the institutions men could devise to protect themselves and preserve order. Human preparations against the immense power of fortune in this sense – like hydraulic engineering – could only limit and channel, not protect against, the resulting damage. Sometimes, like a capricious goddess, fortune simply changed conditions on the playing field, making delay the advisable tactic, even though the individual at the time in question, doomed by his character, would continue to hurl himself forwards against all opponents and destroy himself by doing so. In general, Machiavelli insisted, the bold would succeed better than the hesitant. Fortune, he wrote, framing an image often cited in his own time and still notorious now, was after all a woman. Accordingly she favoured those bold enough to treat her roughly.

Machiavelli's advice about how to deal with fortune was his own. But in his passionate concern with the power of conditions to shape events, and his sense of the fragility of human leaders and their plans, he drew on the intellectual resources of the Florentine ruling class. Patricians whose prominence rested not on ancient birth and military prowess but on sales and investments knew that they could lose everything overnight. Some of them – like the great patron of architecture Giovanni Rucellai – showed an almost obsessive concern with the subject. Rucellai took as his emblem a full sail, indicating that fortune, which could also mean a powerful wind, was pushing the ship of his estate along. He blazoned it everywhere on the great building projects he supported, including the façade of the church of Sta Maria Novella, with its incongruous vista of full sails. And he placed a figure of fortune herself – female, nude and hard to control – on a fine medallion in the courtyard of his Florentine palace. Writers like Leon Battista Alberti regularly invoked the power of fortune to destroy, as well as to support, great families. In treating success and failure as something not earned by good conduct but wrested from the control of an unsympathetic cosmos, Machiavelli used a well-established set of images and metaphors.

Oddly enough, for one who insisted so often on his ability to give a true and profound account of politics, Machiavelli sometimes wrote as if he accepted another, divergent strain in Florentine political thinking. Both Vettori, with whom he collaborated so actively in the period that led up to the writing of *The Prince*, and Francesco Guicciardini, another close friend and sharp critic of Machiavelli, insisted that their friend was often too clever by half. Political intentions were often inscrutable. Political actions often had incalculable effects. And most situations – so Guicciardini argued in his famous *Ricordi* – were simply too different in character for any clear inference to be drawn about the common factors that operated in them. Politics, in short, could not be predicted and controlled, at least not with the devastating simplicity promised by the author of *The Prince*.

For all his self-assuredness as a counsellor, Machiavelli did not wholly disagree with these critics. Men, he admitted, had fixed characters: brave or cowardly, bold or hesitant. Sometimes circumstances might favour one style of action, sometimes another. But no man could always, or often, tailor his character to the changing times. To that extent, all politicians were doomed to failure some of the time, even if bold policies were generally preferable. Machiavelli nowhere sounded more Florentine than when he despaired of the possibility of finding rulers who could put his political observations into practice.

Yet Machiavelli's book, and his political thinking, also departed, in crucial ways, from the traditions of political language which taught him so much. And these departures continue to challenge all interpreters of his life and thought. In the first place, as we have seen, Florence was traditionally a republic; Machiavelli himself had served the republic faithfully, and in the prefatory letter to *The Prince* he even stated that he had discussed republican governments in another work – a remark usually taken as referring to his *Discourses on Livy*, in which he analysed the experience of early Rome in order to work out what institutions could preserve a republic. In *The Prince*, Machiavelli explained how an absolute ruler could take over and maintain control in a previously republican state. In *The Discourses* – a work which, in its final form, reflects lectures Machiavelli gave to a circle of nobles and intellectuals in the pleasant gardens of the Rucellai family, a few years after the fall of the Republic – he tried to explain how the Romans had successfully created and maintained a state with strong popular elements, which existed for centuries.

Though Machiavelli's analysis of republican politics was as tough-minded and pragmatic as his handbook for princes, his later work shows a strong preference for popular government, a belief in the general faithfulness and virtue of the people, that seem hard to reconcile with the hard-headed analysis of the fickle, easily deceived crowd that underpinned his instructions for effective princely behaviour. Many scholars have tried, with varying degrees of success, to reconcile the two works, to explain the differences between them by the development of Machiavelli's thought, or to prove that only one of them reflected his true opinion. However, all such efforts remain indecisive. The nature of Machiavelli's personal ideals – and the way he himself would have compared or contrasted his two works – remains uncertain. Anyone who wishes to deal with the full development of Machiavelli's thought must, above all, explain what this loyal servant of the republic meant by his praise of tyranny.[12]

Even within *The Prince* Machiavelli challenged his readers with problems of interpretation. He insisted, as all readers of his book immediately see, that the prince must employ any tactics, even vicious ones, needed to ensure his control over the state. Terror tactics; the employment of brutal subordinates, who could be executed with brutality themselves once they had carried out their tasks; even the mass murder of one's opponents – all of these expedients appear in the pages of *The Prince*, usually described with apparent equanimity. Machiavelli even made one of the most frightening secular rulers of his time – Cesare Borgia – a kind of hero, not for his virtuous conduct, but for the brilliant combination of tactics which had almost made him the absolute ruler of central Italy. At times, Machiavelli seems to glory in the brutality he describes. Some readers – noting that in real life, as an envoy assigned to Cesare Borgia, Machiavelli had sharply criticized him – have gone so far in their desire to save Machiavelli from the charge of political immorality as to argue that he must have meant to offer not a serious account but a bitter satire on contemporary political life, one that his readers could decode. Many more, from Machiavelli's own time

to the present, have reacted in a radically different way, treating him
as a deliberate teacher of immorality: one whose work signals the
end of one traditional form of political life and thought and the birth
of modernity, with all its characteristic vices. Yet Machiavelli himself,
in other moods, admitted that a ruler could not slaughter his fellow
citizens indiscriminately even if doing so proved effective. Agathocles, the tyrant of Syracuse, could not be called 'virtuous', he
wrote, even if his policies succeeded.

Machiavelli, as Victoria Kahn has shown,[13] thus underlined the
complexity and fluidity of political life and political judgement. He
tried to teach his readers that they must not look for hard-and-fast
rules, but learn to think their way subtly into each different political
situation and its requirements. In insisting that no single quality could
be identified as 'virtue' and pursued in every situation, Machiavelli
became the political teacher of Europe. Generations of readers in
courts and universities learned from him to scrutinize the making
of political decisions with a hard new realism and a clear sense that
some forms of deceit are not to be avoided by any ruler who hopes
to survive. Machiavelli gave his name to the 'Machiavell', the schemer
who manipulated others in Jacobean tragedies, but he also provided
the core of the doctrines of 'reason of state' that became the basic
political education of modern Europe.[14]

Machiavelli hated 'unarmed prophets' (*profeti disarmati*) like
Savonarola. Yet he himself was armed only with a pen when he
became the prophet of a new understanding of politics. He gave
permanent, unforgettable literary form to the sharp, unforgiving
vision of politics that had long been cultivated by members of the
Florentine élite. At the same time, however, he made clear the
limitations of that inherited vision, as well as those of the more
idealistic one that had previously dominated political literature. No
wonder that his portrait of the prince, like Savonarola's, retains its
power to fascinate, to frighten and to instruct.

Notes

1. See Donald Weinstein, *Savonarola and Florence: Prophecy and Patriotism in the Renaissance* (Princeton, 1970).

2. See e.g. Hans Baron, *In Search of Florentine Civic Humanism* (Princeton, 1988).

3. For an introduction to these events, as experienced in Florence, see Mark Phillips, *The Memoir of Marco Parenti: A Life in Medici Florence* (Princeton, 1987).

4. See Weinstein.

5. On Machiavelli's career see Robert Black, 'Machiavelli, Servant of the Florentine Republic', *Machiavelli and Republicanism*, ed. G. Bock, Q. Skinner and M. Viroli (Cambridge, 1990), 72–8.

6. See the fine analysis of John Najemy, *Between Friends: Discourses of Power and Desire in the Machiavelli– Vettori Letters of 1513–1515* (Princeton, 1993).

7. *The Portable Machiavelli*, ed. and tr. P. Bondanella and M. Musa (Penguin, 1979), 69.

8. Felix Gilbert, 'The Humanist Concept of the Prince and *The Prince* of Machiavelli', *History: Choice and Commitment* (Cambridge, Mass., and London, 1977), 91–114.

9. Marcia Colish, 'Cicero's *De officiis* and Machiavelli's *Prince*', *Sixteenth Century Journal* 9 (1978) 91–4.

10. F. Gilbert, *Machiavelli and Guicciardini: Politics and History in Sixteenth-Century Florence* (Princeton, 1965), part I.

11. Ibid.

12. The best introduction into this large subject remains Quentin Skinner, *Foundations of Modern Political Thought* (Cambridge, 1978), vol. I.

13. Victoria Kahn, *Machiavellian Rhetoric: From the Counter-Reformation to Milton* (Princeton, 1994).

14. Ibid.

TRANSLATOR'S NOTE

The Prince is a classic because of its shrewd psychological insight, its prophetic quality, and its hard, vehement prose, and because it has never lost the power to shock. The artist in Machiavelli, as much as the analyst, is often responsible for the shocks. He loved antithesis and generalization; he was intuitive rather than logical; he constantly dramatized his remarks and exaggerated his conclusions for the sake of impact.

The language of *The Prince* is not as modern as many of its sentiments, and I have not tried to modernize it unduly. For example, I have preferred to translate *principe*, in the title and the text, literally as *prince*, rather than lose the associations the word has acquired through the centuries, although for the sake of variation I have used another word, such as ruler, here and there. On the other hand, I have tried to put Machiavelli into clear, unambiguous English, and therefore sometimes shortened his periods and made use of the variety of near synonyms available in English to avoid monotony. The same words and phrases are repeated frequently in all Machiavelli's writings, words like *ambizione, onore, gloria, fortuna, necessità, virtù*. These are key words, both for Machiavelli and other Renaissance writers. They are often, too, employed very judiciously, as, for example, in Chapter VIII of *The Prince*, where Machiavelli uses the word *onore* again and again with mounting irony to describe how Oliverotto tricked his uncle. But I think it dangerous to build too much on these few words or, when translating, to follow too slavishly the rule that one word should always be translated by the same word. In the case of *virtù*, to labour the point, I have decided to translate mostly by the rather literary word 'prowess', but have not hesitated to use quite another word where the context would not admit prowess. A great deal has been written about the Renaissance concept of *virtù*, but Machiavelli, like his contemporaries, seems to have used it freely and loosely, nearly always in antithesis to *fortuna*, sometimes with the sense of willpower, sometimes efficiency, sometimes even with the sense of virtue. (For extensive discussion of key words in Machiavelli's thought see Machiavelli: The Prince edited by Quentin Skinner and Russell Price (Cambridge 1988) pp. 100–113.)

The reader will, I hope, appreciate some of the force of Machiavelli's style in the translation which follows. It is a lean, often colloquial prose, spontaneous and direct, capable of sharp bitterness and irony – as in the chapter on Ecclesiastical Principalities – but also of impressive rhetoric. *The Prince* is constructed fairly formally – the chapter headings, for instance, were set down in Latin,[1] and some of it may today seem narrow and remote although continually one is startled by its modern applicability. It was written by a man of strong and complex passions and the writing faithfully mirrors the exciting thoughts of an imaginative intelligence.

The text I have mostly relied on is that published in Florence in 1929 and edited by Mazzoni and Casella.

I have, finally, many debts to acknowledge: to the late Dr E. V. Rieu, for his advice and kindness, to John Hale for invaluable guidance, to Martin Judge, who helped me with my English, and Guido Waldman and the late Peter Tumiati, who helped with my Italian, and to Dr Russell Price, who has generously shared with me the fruits of his own scholarship from the study of translations of Machiavelli, and several of whose suggested readings I have been glad to follow.

I am especially indebted to the late Professor J. H. Whitfield for generously suggesting some of the changes made in the 1975 and subsequent editions of this translation. His readily given advice has substantially improved the fidelity of the translation to Machiavelli's thoughts.

G. B.

SELECTED BOOKS

For the reader who wants to consult an Italian text of *The Prince*, the most suitable is published by Feltrinelli (Milan) in the volume of the *Opere* containing *Il Principe e Discorsi*. *Niccolò Machiavelli: An Annotated Bibliography of Modern Criticism and Scholarship* compiled by Silvia Ruffo Fiore (Greenwood Press 1990) provides a valuable annotated source for research on scholarship and criticism published on Machiavelli between 1935 and 1985 with an appendix (not annotated) citing research published after 1985.

Recommended for further reading are:

The Life and Times of Niccolò Machiavelli by Pasquale Villari (translated into English by Linda Villari, various editions in Italian and English following the 1877–82 three-volume Italian text).

Il Principe edited by L. Burd (Oxford 1891; reprinted 1968) with a remarkable Introduction by Lord Acton and useful historical notes.

Machiavelli by J. H. Whitfield (Blackwell 1947)

The Statecraft of Machiavelli by H. Butterfield (Bell 1955)

Machiavelli and the Renaissance by F. Chabod (trs. David Moore, Bowes and Bowes 1958)

The Literary Works of Machiavelli by J. R. Hale, translations of selected letters and the plays *Mandragola* and *Clizia* (Oxford 1961)

Machiavelli and Renaissance Italy by J. R. Hale (English University Press 1961)

Life of Niccolò Machiavelli by R. Ridolfi (trs. C. Grayson, Routledge & Kegan Paul 1963)

The English Face of Machiavelli by Felix Raab (Routledge & Kegan Paul 1964)

Selected Books

Machiavelli and Guicciardini by Felix Gilbert (Princeton 1965)

Machiavelli: A Dissection by Sydney Anglo (Gollancz 1969)

Discourses on Machiavelli by J. H. Whitfield (Heffer 1969)

Against the Current by Isaiah Berlin, collected essays with 'The Originality of Machiavelli' (Hogarth Press 1979)

Machiavelli by Quentin Skinner (Oxford 1981)

Machiavelli and Mystery of State by Peter S. Donaldson (Cambridge 1988)

Machiavelli in Hell by Sebastian de Grazia (Harvester Wheatsheaf 1989)

Machiavelli and Republicanism, ed. G. Bock, Q. Skinner and M. Viroli (Cambridge 1990)

From Politics to Reason of State by M. Viroli (Cambridge 1992)

Machiavelli and the Discourse of Literature ed. by Albert Russell Ascoli and Victoria Kahn (Cornell 1993)

Between Friends: Discourses of Power and Desire in the Machiavelli– Vettori Letters of 1513–1515, ed. by John M. Najemy (Princeton University Press, 1993)

MACHIAVELLI'S
PRINCIPAL WORKS

1499 *Discorso della guerra di Pisa*
Report on the Pisan war

1503 *Descrizione del modo tenuto dal Duca Valentino nell' ammazzare*
Vitellozzo Vitelli, Oliverotto da Fermo, il signor Pagolo e il Duca
di Gravina Orsini
Description of the Manner in which Duke Valentino put
Vitellozzo Vitelli, Oliverotto da Fermo, Lord Pagolo and the
Duke of Gravina Orsini to Death

1503 *Parole sopra la provvisione del danaio*
Remarks on the raising of money

1503 *Del modo di trattare i sudditi della Valdichiana ribellati*
On the method of dealing with the rebels of the Val di Chiana

1504 *Decennale Primo*
The First Decade

1506 *Discorso dell'ordinare lo stato di Firenze alle armi*
Discourse on Florentine military preparation

1508 *Rapporto delle cose dell' Alemagna*
Report on Germany

1509 *Discorso sopra le cose della Magna e sopra lo imperatore*
Discourse on Germany and the Emperor

[1509]   *Decennale Secondo*
      The Second Decade

[after April 1512]   *Ritratto delle cose della Magna*
      Description of German affairs

[after April 1512 and before August 1513]   *Ritratto delle cose di Francia*
      Description of French affairs

1513   *Il Principe*
      The Prince

1515–16–17   *Discorsi sopra la prima deca di Tito Livio*
      Discourses on the First Decade of Livy

[1514 or later]   *Discorso o dialogo intorno alla nostra lingua*
      Discourse or dialogue on our language

[1517 or 18]   *L'Asino d'oro*
      The Golden Ass

1518   *Mandragola*
      The Mandrake Root

[1515–20]   *Belfagor*
      Belfagor

1519–20   *Dell' Arte della Guerra*
      The Art of War

1520 *Sommario delle cose della città di Lucca*
      Summary of Lucchese affairs

1520 *La vita di Castruccio Castracani da Lucca*
      The Life of Castruccio Castracani of Lucca

1519 or 1520 *Discorso delle cose fiorentine dopo la morte di Lorenzo*
      Discourse on the Florentine affairs after the death of Lorenzo

Begun 1520 finished 1525 *Istorie Fiorentine*
      The History of Florence

1522 *Memoriale a Raffaello Girolami*
      Advice to Raffaello Girolami

[1524–5] *Clizia*
      Clizia

1526 *Relazione di una visita fatta per fortificare Firenze*
      Report on the fortifications of Florence

(Dates in square brackets are conjectural)

Letter from NICCOLÒ MACHIAVELLI TO THE
MAGNIFICENT LORENZO DÉ MEDICI[1]

Men who are anxious to win the favour of a Prince nearly always follow the custom of presenting themselves to him with the possessions they value most, or with things they know especially please him; so we often see princes given horses, weapons, cloth of gold, precious stones, and similar ornaments worthy of their high position. Now, I am anxious to offer myself to Your Magnificence with some token of my devotion to you, and I have not found among my belongings anything as dear to me or that I value as much as my understanding of the deeds of great men, won by me from a long acquaintance with contemporary affairs and a continuous study of the ancient world; these matters I have very diligently analysed and pondered for a long time, and now, having summarized them in a little book, I am sending them to Your Magnificence.

And although I consider this work unworthy to be put before you, yet I am fully confident that you will be kind enough to accept it, seeing that I could not give you a more valuable gift than the means of being able in a very short space of time to grasp all that I, over so many years and with so much affliction and peril, have learned and understood. I have not embellished or crammed this book with rounded periods or big, impressive words, or with any blandishment or superfluous decoration of the kind which many are in the habit of using to describe or adorn what they have produced; for my ambition has been either that nothing should distinguish my book, or that it should find favour solely through the variety of its contents and the seriousness of its subject-matter. Nor I hope will it be considered presumptuous for a man of low and humble status to dare discuss and lay down the law about how princes should rule; because, just as men who are sketching the landscape put themselves down in the plain to study the nature of the mountains and the highlands, and to study the low-lying land they put themselves high on the mountains, so, to comprehend fully the nature of the people, one must be a prince, and to comprehend fully the nature of princes one must be an ordinary citizen.

So, Your Magnificence, take this little gift in the spirit in which I send it; and if you read and consider it diligently, you will discover in it my urgent wish that you reach the eminence that fortune and your other qualities promise you. And if, from your lofty peak, Your Magnificence will sometimes glance down to these low-lying regions, you will realize the extent to which, undeservedly, I have to endure the great and unremitting malice of fortune.

Call for employment

The Prince

I. *How many kinds of principality there are and the ways in which they are acquired*

All the states, all the dominions under whose authority men have lived in the past and live now have been and are either republics or principalities. Principalities are hereditary, with their prince's family long established as rulers, or they are new. The new are completely new, as was Milan to Francesco Sforza, or they are like limbs joined to the hereditary state of the prince who acquires them, as is the kingdom of Naples in relation to the king of Spain. Dominions so acquired are accustomed to be under a prince, or used to freedom; a prince wins them either with the arms of others or with his own, either by fortune or by prowess.

II. *Hereditary principalities*

I shall leave out any discussion of republics, since I discussed them at length on another occasion. I shall deal only with the principality, and I shall follow the order set out above, and debate how these principalities can be governed and maintained.

I say, then, that in hereditary states, accustomed to their prince's family, there are far fewer difficulties in maintaining one's rule than in new principalities; because it is enough merely not to neglect the institutions founded by one's ancestors and then to adapt policy to events. In this way, if the prince is reasonably assiduous he will always maintain his rule, unless some extraordinary and inordinate force deprive him of it; and if so deprived, whenever the usurper suffers a setback he will reconquer.

We have in Italy, for example, the duke of Ferrara;[1] he could not withstand the assaults of the Venetians in '84, nor those of Pope Julius in 1510, but for other reasons than that he had been long established. The fact is that the natural prince has less reason and less need to give offence; and so it follows that he should be more loved; and if he does not provoke hatred by extraordinary vices, it stands to reason that his subjects should naturally be well disposed towards him. And in the antiquity and persistence of his rule memories of innovations and the reasons for them disappear; because one change always leaves a toothing-stone[2] for the next.

III. *Composite principalities*

But in the new principality difficulties do arise. First, if it is not entirely new but a new appendage to an old state (so that the territory as a whole can be called composite) disorders arise chiefly because of one natural difficulty always encountered in new principalities. What happens is that men willingly change their ruler, expecting to fare better. This expectation induces them to take up arms against him; but they only deceive themselves, and they learn from experience that they have made matters worse. This follows from another common and natural necessity: a prince is always compelled to injure those who have made him the new ruler, subjecting them to the troops and imposing the endless other hardships which his new conquest entails. As a result you are opposed by all those you have injured in occupying the principality, and you cannot keep the friendship of those who have put you there; you cannot satisfy them in the way they had taken for granted, yet you cannot use strong medicine on them, as you are in their debt. For always, no matter how powerful one's armies, in order to enter a country one needs the goodwill of the inhabitants. It was for these reasons that Louis

XII, king of France, speedily occupied Milan and speedily lost it.[1]
On the first occasion Ludovico's own forces were enough to take
the city from him, because the people who had opened the gates to
him, finding they had deceived themselves in their expectations and
as regards the benefits they had anticipated, could not stand the
affronts they received from the newcomer.

It is certainly true that when lands that have rebelled are recon-
quered they are not lost so easily; for the ruler, taking advantage of
the revolt, is less scrupulous in securing himself by punishing the
offenders, probing suspects, strengthening himself where he is weak-
est. Thus for France to lose Milan all that had to happen the first
time was that a Duke Ludovico should rampage on the borders, but
for France to lose it a second time the whole world had to oppose
her, and her armies had to be destroyed or chased out of Italy; and
the reasons for this I gave above. None the less, both times France
lost Milan.

The general reasons for the first loss have been discussed. It remains
now to give those for the second, and to see what remedies were
available to the king of France, and what steps could have been
taken by someone in the same straits to maintain his conquest more
securely than he did. Now I say that those states which when acquired
are joined to a state long held by the conqueror are either of the
same country, sharing the same language, or they are not. When
they are, it is a very easy matter to hold on to them, especially when
they are not used to freedom; and to hold them securely it is enough
to have destroyed the line of the former ruling prince. For the rest,
so long as their old ways of life are undisturbed and there is no
divergence in customs, men live quietly: as we have seen in the case
of Burgundy, Brittany, Gascony, and Normandy, which have been
with France for so long. Although here there is some divergence in
language, none the less their customs are similar, and they can easily
get along together. If the ruler wants to keep hold of his new
possessions, he must bear two things in mind: first, that the family
of the old prince must be destroyed; next, that he must change

not alienate the population

neither their laws nor their taxes. In this way, in a very short space of time the new principality will be rolled into one with the old.

But when states are acquired in a province differing in language, in customs, and in institutions, then difficulties arise; and to hold them one must be very fortunate and very assiduous. One of the best, most effective expedients would be for the conqueror to go to live there in person. This course of action would make a new possession more secure and more permanent; and this was what the Turk achieved in Greece.[2] For all the other measures he took, had he not gone to settle there he would have found it impossible to hold that state. Being on the spot, one can detect trouble at the start and deal with it immediately; if one is absent, it is discerned only when it has grown serious, and it is then too late. And besides, this policy prevents the conquered territory from being plundered by one's officials. The subjects are satisfied because they have direct recourse to the prince; and so they have more reason to love him, if they want to be good, and to fear him, if they want to be otherwise. Anyone wishing to invade the state has to think twice about it. So if he settles there the ruler can lose his new state only with the greatest difficulty.

options

The other superior expedient is to establish settlements in one or two places; these will, as it were, fetter the state to you. Unless you establish settlements, you will have to garrison large numbers of mounted troops and infantry. Settlements do not cost much, and the prince can found them and maintain them at little or no personal expense. He injures only those from whom he takes land and houses to give to the new inhabitants, and these victims form a tiny minority, and can never do any harm since they remain poor and scattered. All the others are left undisturbed, and so should stay quiet, and as well as this they are frightened to do wrong lest what happened to the dispossessed should happen to them. To sum up, settlements are economical and more faithful, and do less harm; and those who are injured cannot hurt you because, as I said, they are scattered and poor. And here it has to be noted that men must be either pampered or crushed, because they can get revenge for small injuries but not for grievous ones. So any injury a prince does a man should be of such a kind that there is no fear of revenge. If, however, instead of establishing settlements the prince sends in troops, expenses are far higher, as all the revenues have to be devoted to defence and the gain becomes a loss. The prince does far more injury, because he harms the whole state by billeting his army in different parts of the country, everyone suffers from this annoyance, and everybody is turned into an enemy. And those who grow hostile can do him harm, because they remain, defeated, in their own homes. In every way, therefore, this means of defence is as useless as colonization is useful.

In addition, anyone in a country which differs from his own in the way I described should make himself the leader and protector of the smaller neighbouring powers, and he should endeavour to weaken those which are strong. He should also take precautions to check an invasion of the province by a foreigner as powerful as himself. Invariably, the intruder will be brought in by those who are disaffected, because of excessive ambition or because of fear. Thus the Aetolians once brought the Romans into Greece; and in every other country they invaded, the Romans were brought in by the inhabitants. This is what happens: as soon as a powerful foreigner invades a country all the weaker powers give him their support, moved by envy of the power which has so far dominated them. So, as far as these weaker powers are concerned, he has no trouble at all in winning them to his side, because of their own accord they straight away merge with the state he establishes. All he has to watch is that they do not build up too much strength and too much authority; and with his own strength and their support he can easily hold down those who are powerful and so make himself, in everything, the master of the country. Whoever does not attend carefully to these points will quickly lose what he has acquired; even while he still holds on he will experience countless difficulties and annoyances.

The Romans, in the countries they seized, did watch these matters carefully. They established settlements, supported the weaker powers without increasing their strength, crushed the powerful, and did not allow any powerful foreigner to win prestige. The country of Greece provides a good enough example. Here, the Romans supported the Achaeans and the Aetolians; they crushed the Macedonian kingdom; and they drove out Antiochus. They never allowed the Achaeans or the Aetolians to expand their territories however well they behaved; they never allowed Philip to persuade them into an alliance without holding him down; and despite his power, Antiochus was never granted any authority in Greece. In these instances, the Romans did what all wise rulers must: cope not only with present troubles but also with ones likely to arise in future, and assiduously forestall them.. When trouble is sensed well in advance it can easily be remedied; if you wait for it to show itself any medicine will be too late because the disease will have become incurable. As the doctors say of a wasting disease, to start with it is easy to cure but difficult to diagnose; after a time, unless it has been diagnosed and treated at the outset, it becomes easy to diagnose but difficult to cure. So it is in politics. Political disorders can be quickly healed if they are seen well in advance (and only a prudent ruler has such foresight); when, for lack of a diagnosis, they are allowed to grow in such a way that everyone can recognize them, remedies are too late.

So the Romans saw when troubles were coming and always took counter-measures. They never, to avoid a war, allowed them to go unchecked, because they knew that there is no avoiding war; it can only be postponed to the advantage of others. They made up their minds to wage war with Philip and Antiochus in Greece,[3] in order not to have to do so in Italy. At the time they could have avoided doing either, but they would not. Nor were the Romans ever tempted to do what we hear every day on the lips of the wise men of our generation, to make the most of the present time; rather, they made the most of their own prowess and prudence. Time sweeps everything along and can bring good as well as evil, evil as well as good.

But let us go back to France, and see if that country has adopted any of the measures I have been discussing. I shall talk about Louis, not Charles, and so about a man whose career it has been possible to study more closely because he was entrenched in Italy for a longer time. You will see how Louis has done the opposite of what ought to be done to maintain one's rule in an alien country.[4]

King Louis was brought into Italy by the ambition of the Venetians, who wanted by this means to win for themselves half Lombardy. I do not mean to condemn the course of action taken by the king; he wanted to get a footing in Italy, he had no allies there – on the contrary because of the actions of King Charles all the gates were barred to him – and so he was forced to make friends where he could. His policy in this matter would even have proved successful, provided he had not gone wrong elsewhere. Now, when Lombardy fell into his hands the king immediately regained the standing which Charles had lost. Genoa capitulated; the Florentines became his allies; the marquis of Mantua, the duke of Ferrara, the Bentivogli, the countess of Forlì, the rulers of Faenza, of Pesaro, of Rimini, of Camerino, of Piombino,[5] the citizens of Lucca, Pisa, Siena, all came forward to seek his friendship. Then the Venetians were in a position to realize how rash they had been. In order to gain two towns in Lombardy they had made him, the king, ruler of a third of Italy.

Now consider with what little trouble the king could have maintained his standing in Italy, if he had observed the rules I gave above and kept all those allies of his safe and secure. There were many of them, and they were weak and frightened, some of the Church, some of the Venetians; so they were bound to stay by him, and through them he could easily have safeguarded himself against the powers which remained strong. But no sooner was he in Milan than he did the contrary, helping Pope Alexander to occupy the Romagna. Nor did he realize that by taking this decision he weakened himself, alienated his allies and those who had thrown themselves into his arms, and strengthened the Church by adding so much temporal power to its existing spiritual power, which gives it such authority.

Having made one mistake, he was forced to make others. To frustrate the ambition of Alexander and prevent his becoming ruler of Tuscany he was forced to come down into Italy himself. Not content with having made the Church powerful and having alienated his allies, he then, because he wanted the kingdom of Naples, divided it with the king of Spain.[6] Whereas to start with he was master of Italy he now brought in a rival to whom the ambitious and the discontented might have recourse. He could have left in Naples a king who was in his pay.[7] Instead he expelled him to put in his place one who could chase him out in turn.

The wish to acquire more is admittedly a very natural and common thing; and when men succeed in this they are always praised rather than condemned. But when they lack the ability to do so and yet want to acquire more at all costs, they deserve condemnation for their mistakes. If France could have attacked Naples with her own forces, she should have done so; if not, she should not have divided it. And if the partition of Lombardy with the Venetians could be excused, because it gave Louis a foothold in Italy, the other partition deserved to be condemned, because there was no such necessity for it.

Louis had, therefore, made these five mistakes: he had destroyed the weaker powers; increased the power of someone already powerful in Italy; brought into that country a very powerful foreigner; stayed away from Italy himself; failed to establish settlements there. Even these mistakes, if he had lived, need not have been fatal if there had not been a sixth: his dispossessing the Venetians of their state.[8] If he had not made the Church strong, or brought Spain into Italy, it would have been reasonable and necessary to crush the Venetians. But having taken those steps, he should never have let them be ruined; because while they remained powerful they would always have prevented the others from moving against Lombardy. The Venetians would have opposed this unless it gave them control of Lombardy themselves, and the others would not have wanted to wrest it from France to give it to them. Nor would they have had the courage to defy both France and the Venetians. If anyone should say that King

Louis ceded the Romagna[9] to Alexander and the kingdom of Naples to Spain in order to escape a war, I would reply with the arguments used above, that one must never allow disorder to continue so as to escape a war. Anyhow one does not escape: the war is merely postponed to one's disadvantage. And if anyone should cite the king's good faith, which he had pledged to the pope, and his promise to undertake that enterprise in return for having his marriage dissolved and a cardinal's hat given to Rouen, my reply is what I shall say later concerning the good faith of princes and the way they should keep their word. King Louis, therefore, lost Lombardy because he observed none of the rules observed by others who have seized countries and determined to hold on to them. There is nothing fantastic about this, it is very commonplace and reasonable. I had a word on this subject with Rouen, at Nantes, when Valentino (as Cesare Borgia, son of Pope Alexander, was popularly called) was occupying the Romagna. When the cardinal of Rouen said to me that the Italians did not understand war, I retorted that the French did not understand statecraft, because, if they understood it, then they would not let the Church become so great. And the course of events in Italy has shown how the greatness of the Church and of Spain has been caused by France, and how the ruin of France has been caused by them. From this we can deduce a general rule, which never or rarely fails to apply: that whoever is responsible for another's becoming powerful ruins himself, because this power is brought into being either by ingenuity or by force, and both of these are suspect to the one who has become powerful.

IV. *Why the kingdom of Darius conquered by Alexander did not rebel against his successors after his death*

One could well wonder, after having considered all the difficulties involved in holding a newly acquired state, how it was that when Alexander, who had in a few years become ruler of all Asia, died with his conquest scarcely completed, there was not, as might have been expected, a general uprising.[1] Instead, Alexander's successors ruled securely; and in their government the only difficulty arose from their own ambitions and rivalries. My answer to this problem is that all principalities known to history are governed in one of two ways, either by a prince to whom everyone is subservient and whose ministers, with his favour and permission, help govern, or by a prince and by nobles whose rank is established not by favour of the prince but by their ancient lineage. Such nobles have states and subjects of their own, and these acknowledge them as their lords and bear a natural affection towards them. In states governed by a prince and his servants, the prince has greater authority. For throughout the whole country he alone is recognized as being entitled to allegiance; anyone else is obeyed as a minister and an official for whom no special love is felt.

Contemporary examples of these two different kinds of government are provided by the Turk and the king of France. The Turkish empire is ruled by one man; all the others are his servants. This one ruler divides the empire into *sandjaks*,[2] in charge of which he places various administrators, whom he changes and varies as it suits him. But the king of France is surrounded by a long-established order of nobles, who are acknowledged in France by their own subjects and are loved by them. They have their prerogatives; the king cannot take these away from them except at his own peril. So, to make a comparison between these two kinds of state, it is difficult to win control of the Turkish empire but, once it has been conquered, it can be held with ease. On the other hand, in several respects you will find that the French state can be more easily seized, but it can be held only with great difficulty.

The reasons for it being difficult to succeed in winning possession of the Turkish empire are that there is no chance of being called in by the local princes, and that one cannot hope to forward the enterprise by the rebellion of those who are near to the ruler. And this is because of the reasons I gave above: they are all slaves bound in loyalty to their master and so it is more difficult to corrupt them; and even should they be corrupted one cannot hope to make much use of them because they are unable, for the reasons already given, to draw the people after them. Whoever attacks the Turkish empire, therefore, must expect to find it completely united, and he is constrained to base his hopes on his own strength rather than his enemy's disunity. But if once the Turk has been vanquished and broken in battle so that he cannot raise new armies, there is nothing to worry about except the ruler's family. When that has been wiped out there is no one left to fear, because the others have no credit with the people; and just as before his victory the conqueror has nothing to hope from them, so afterwards he need not fear them.

The opposite happens in kingdoms governed in the way France is. You can easily invade if you win over one of the barons. There always exist malcontents and those who want a change. These, for the reasons explained, can open up the state to you and facilitate your victory. But subsequently, when you want to maintain your rule, you run into countless difficulties, as regards both those who have helped you and those you have subjugated. Nor is it enough for you to destroy the ruler's family, because there still remain nobles to raise insurrections; and being able neither to satisfy them nor to destroy them you lose the state as soon as their opportunity presents itself.

Now, if you will consider the kind of government which Darius administered, you will find it resembled that of the Turk; and so first of all Alexander had to attack him head-on and drive him from the field. Then, after he had won that victory and Darius was dead, the state rested securely in Alexander's hands for the reasons discussed above. Had they been united, his successors could have enjoyed it undisturbed; certainly, there were no tumults other than those they themselves provoked. But as for states constituted like France, it is impossible to rule them with so little trouble. This fact explains the many rebellions against the Romans in Spain, France, and Greece, which were due to the number of principalities of which these countries were composed. The Romans were always unsure of their hold while the memory of these principalities endured. But when Roman rule had been long established and had become powerful, and the principalities were completely forgotten, the Romans consolidated their position. Later on, however, when they, the Romans, fought among themselves,[3] each one of them could draw support from various parts of the conquered territories in proportion to the authority he had acquired; allegiance was given to the Romans individually because the families of the former rulers had been wiped out. So if this is borne in mind no one will wonder at the ease with which Alexander kept command of Asia, or at the difficulties encountered by others, such as Pyrrhus and many more like him, in maintaining their conquests. This contrast does not depend on whether the conquerors are more or less capable but on the kind of state they conquer.

limits that cannot be altered. Imponderables.

v. *How cities or principalities which lived under their own laws should be administered after being conquered*

When states newly acquired as I said have been accustomed to living freely under their own laws, there are three ways to hold them securely: first, by devastating them; next, by going and living there in person; thirdly, by letting them keep their own laws, exacting tribute, and setting up an oligarchy which will keep the state friendly to you. In the last case, the government will know that it cannot endure without the friendship and power of the prince who created it, and so it has to exert itself to maintain his authority. A city used to freedom can be more easily ruled through its own citizens, provided you do not wish to destroy it, than in any other way.

Examples are provided by the Spartans and the Romans. The Spartans ruled Athens and Thebes through the oligarchies they established there, although in the end they lost them.[1] The Romans, in order to hold Capua, Carthage, and Numantia, destroyed them, and so never lost them.[2] They wanted to rule Greece almost as the Spartans did, freely, under its own laws, but they did not succeed; so in order to maintain their power they were constrained to destroy many cities in that province. Indeed, there is no surer way of keeping possession than by devastation. Whoever becomes the master of a city accustomed to freedom, and does not destroy it, may expect to be destroyed himself; because, when there is a rebellion, such a city justifies itself by calling on the name of liberty and its ancient institutions, never forgotten despite the passing of time and the benefits received from the new ruler. Whatever the conqueror's actions or foresight, if the inhabitants are not dispersed and scattered, they will forget neither that name nor those institutions; and at the first opportunity they will at once have recourse to them, as did Pisa[3] after having been kept in servitude for a hundred years by the Florentines. But when cities or provinces are used to living under a prince, and his family is wiped out, since on the one hand they are used to obeying, and on the other have lost their former prince, they cannot agree on the choice of a new prince from among themselves and they cannot live in freedom without one. So they are slower to take up arms, and a prince can win them and assure himself of them more easily. But in republics there is more life, more hatred, a greater desire for revenge; the memory of their ancient liberty does not and cannot let them rest; in their case the surest way is to wipe them out or to live there in person.

VI. *New principalities acquired by one's own arms and prowess*

No one should be surprised if, in discussing states where both the prince and the constitution are new, I shall give the loftiest examples. Men nearly always follow the tracks made by others and proceed in their affairs by imitation, even though they cannot entirely keep to the tracks of others or emulate the prowess of their models. So a prudent man must always follow in the footsteps of great men and imitate those who have been outstanding. If his own prowess fails to compare with theirs, at least it has an air of greatness about it. He must behave like those archers who, if they are skilful, when the target seems too distant, know the capabilities of their bow and aim a good deal higher than their objective, not in order to shoot so high but so that by aiming high they can reach the target.

I say, therefore, that in completely new states, where the prince himself is a newcomer, the difficulty he encounters in maintaining his rule is more or less serious insofar as he is more or less able. And since the very fact that from being a private citizen he has become a prince presupposes either ability or good fortune, it would seem that one or the other of these should to some extent lessen many of the difficulties encountered. None the less, the less a man has relied on fortune the stronger he has made his position. It also helps if the prince has no other states and so is forced to live in his new state in person. But to come to those who became princes by their own abilities and not by good fortune, I say that the most outstanding are Moses, Cyrus, Romulus, Theseus, and others like them.[1] Although one should not reason about Moses, since he merely executed what God commanded, yet he must be praised for the grace which made him worthy of speaking with God. But let us consider Cyrus and the others who acquired and founded kingdoms: they were all praiseworthy, and their actions and institutions, when examined, do not seem to differ from those of Moses, who had such a mighty teacher. And when we come to examine their actions and lives, they do not seem to have had from fortune anything other than opportunity. Fortune, as it were, provided the matter but they gave it its form; without opportunity their prowess would have been extinguished, and without such prowess the opportunity would have come in vain.

Thus for the Israelites to be ready to follow Moses, in order to escape from servitude, it was necessary for him to find them, in Egypt, enslaved and oppressed by the Egyptians. For Romulus to become king of Rome and founder of his country, he had to have left Alba and been exposed to die when he was born. Cyrus needed to find the Persians rebellious against the empire of the Medes, and the Medes grown soft and effeminate through the long years of peace. Theseus could not have demonstrated his prowess had he not found the Athenians dispersed. The opportunities given them enabled these men to succeed, and their own exceptional prowess enabled them to seize their opportunities; in consequence their countries were ennobled and enjoyed great prosperity.

Men who become rulers by prowess similar to theirs acquire their principalities with difficulty but hold them with ease. The difficulties they encounter in acquiring their principalities arise partly because of the new institutions and laws they are forced to introduce in founding the state and making themselves secure. It should be borne in mind that there is nothing more difficult to handle, more doubtful of success, and more dangerous to carry through than initiating changes in a state's constitution. The innovator makes enemies of all those who prospered under the old order, and only lukewarm support is forthcoming from those who would prosper under the new. Their support is lukewarm partly from fear of their adversaries, who have the existing laws on their side, and partly because men are generally incredulous, never really trusting new things unless they have tested them by experience. In consequence, whenever those who oppose the changes can do so, they attack vigorously, and the defence made by the others is only lukewarm. So both the innovator and his friends come to grief. But to discuss this subject thoroughly we must distinguish between innovators who stand alone and those who depend on others, that is between those who to achieve their purposes can force the issue and those who must use persuasion. In the second case, they always come to grief, having achieved nothing; when, however, they depend on their own resources and can force the issue, then they are seldom endangered. That is why all armed prophets have conquered, and unarmed prophets have come to grief. Besides what I have said already, the populace is by nature fickle; it is easy to persuade them of something, but difficult to confirm them in that persuasion. Therefore one must urgently arrange matters so that when they no longer believe they can be made to believe by force. Moses, Cyrus, Theseus, and Romulus would not have been able to have their institutions respected a long time if they had been unarmed, as was the case in our time with <u>Frà Girolamo Savonarola</u> who came to grief with his new institutions when the crowd started to lose faith in him, and he had no way of holding fast those who had believed or of forcing the incredulous to believe. Men such as he have considerable difficulty in achieving their ends, and the most dangerous time for them is when they are still striving; but once they have succeeded and begin to be venerated, having destroyed those who were envious of their abilities, they stay powerful, secure, respected, and happy.

I want now to add another, lesser example to these lofty ones. It will, however, bear the comparison to some extent, and I shall let it stand for others of its kind. The example I have in mind is Hiero of Syracuse. From being a private citizen, he became ruler of Syracuse. He too owed nothing to fortune except his opportunity, because the Syracusans chose him to lead their army when they were being driven hard, and then he earned the right to be their prince.[2] His prowess was such, even when he was an ordinary citizen, that his biographer wrote: '*quod nihil illi deerat ad regnandum praeter regnum*'.[3] He disbanded the old militia and organized a new one; he abandoned former alliances and made fresh ones; and when he had his own alliances and troops he had the foundations for whatever he wanted. Hiero, therefore, had <u>to work very hard to establish his position</u>, but very little to <u>maintain it.</u>

VII. *New principalities acquired with the help of fortune and foreign arms*

Private citizens who become princes purely by good fortune do so with little exertion on their own part; but subsequently they maintain their position only by considerable exertion. They make the journey as if they had wings; their problems start when they alight. This is the case with men who either buy their way into power or are granted it by the favour of someone else, as happened with many in Greece, in the cities of Ionia and the Hellespont, who were made satraps by Darius so that they might rule those cities for his security and glory. This was also the case with those who from being private citizens became emperors by corrupting the soldiers. Such rulers rely on the goodwill and fortune of those who have elevated them, and both these are capricious, unstable things. They do not know how to maintain their position, and they cannot do so. They do not know how, because, unless they possess considerable talent and prowess, private citizens are incapable of commanding; they cannot, because they do not have loyal and devoted troops of their own. Then again, governments set up overnight, like everything in nature whose growth is forced, lack strong roots and ramifications. So they are destroyed in the first bad spell. This is inevitable unless those who have suddenly become princes are of such prowess that overnight they can learn how to preserve what fortune has suddenly tossed into their laps, and unless they can then lay foundations such as other princes would have already been building on.

Of these two ways of becoming a prince, by prowess or by fortune, I want now to give two examples from living memory: namely Francesco Sforza and Cesare Borgia. Francesco, using the right means, and by his own great prowess, from being a private citizen became duke of Milan. What he won only after endless struggles he then held with little exertion. On the other hand, Cesare Borgia, commonly called duke Valentino, acquired his state through the good fortune of his father, and lost it when that disappeared; and this happened even though he used the same ways and means any prudent and capable prince would to consolidate his power in the states he had won by the arms and fortune of others. As I said before, a man of exceptional prowess can build the foundations of his state after he has acquired it, even if by doing so he runs a risk himself as well as endangering the whole subsequent edifice. So if we consider the duke's career as a whole, we find that he laid strong foundations for the future. And I do not consider it superfluous to discuss these, because I know no better precepts to give a new prince than ones derived from Cesare's actions; and if what he instituted was of no avail, this was not his fault but arose from the extraordinary and inordinate malice of fortune.

Alexander VI, when he sought the aggrandizement of his son, faced a considerable number of actual and potential difficulties. First, he saw no way of acquiring a state for the duke, unless it were one of the states of the Church; but he knew the duke of Milan[1] and the Venetians would never consent if he set out to seize one of these. Faenza and Rimini were already under the protection of the Venetians. He saw as well that the Italian arms, or such of them as he could hope to utilize, were controlled by those who had reason to fear the aggrandizement of the pope; he could not trust himself to them, since they belonged to the Orsini and the Colonna and their confederates. What he had to do, therefore, was to create disorder, throwing their states into a turmoil, so that he could win secure control of part of them. This proved very easy to do because he found the Venetians, for other reasons, endeavouring to bring the French back into Italy. Not only did Alexander not gainsay this, he facilitated it by dissolving King Louis' former marriage. So the king invaded Italy with the help of the Venetians and the consent of Alexander, and he was no sooner in Milan than the pope had troops from him for the Romagna campaign; and the Romagna yielded to him because of the standing of the king in Italy. But then when the duke had won the Romagna,[2] and the Colonna had been crushed, two things prevented him from consolidating his position and advancing further: first, the loyalty of his troops was doubtful, and second, there was the policy of France. To explain this, it seemed that the Orsini troops, of which he had made use, might betray him, not only halting his progress but robbing him of what he had won; and it seemed that the king might do the same. He had one confirmation of these fears when, after the capture of Faenza, he assaulted Bologna and saw the Orsini troops go into battle half-heartedly. As for the king, the duke realized what was in his mind when, after capturing the duchy of Urbino, he invaded Tuscany and the king called him off. So the duke determined to rely no longer on the arms and fortune of others. First he undermined the power of the Orsini and Colonna factions in Rome, winning the allegiance of all their high-born adherents by giving them offices and commissions, and honouring them according to their rank. The upshot was that within a few months their attachment to the factions was destroyed and they were all for the duke. After this he waited his chance to destroy the leaders of the Orsini, having already dispersed those of the Colonna. A good opportunity came his way, and he used it well. What happened was that the Orsini realized, belatedly, that the aggrandizement of the duke and of the Church spelled their own ruin, and therefore they summoned a conference at Magione near Perugia. Out of this meeting came the revolt of Urbino, uprisings in the Romagna, and countless dangers to the duke. He overcame all of these with the help of the French. His former standing in Italy was restored, but he no longer trusted France or the forces of others, and in order not to run risks by doing so he turned to stratagem. His powers of dissimulation were so great that even the Orsini, through Signor Paulo, reconciled themselves with him. The duke used every device of diplomacy to reassure Paulo, giving him gifts of money, clothes, and horses; and so their simplicity led the Orsini to Sinigaglia, into his hands. So, the leaders destroyed, their followers were forced into the duke's camp. The duke had laid excellent foundations for his future power. He held all the Romagna with the duchy of Urbino, and, above all, he seemed to have won the trust and friendship of the Romagna and its inhabitants, now that they had started to prosper under his rule.

As this point deserves close study and imitation by others, I will not leave it out. Now, the duke won control of the Romagna and found that it had previously been ruled by weak overlords, quicker to despoil their subjects than to govern them well. They had given them cause for anarchy rather than union, to such an extent that the province was rife with brigandage, factions, and every sort of abuse. He decided therefore that it needed good government to pacify it and make it obedient to the sovereign authority. So he placed there messer Remirro de Orco, a cruel, efficient man, to whom he entrusted the fullest powers. In a short time this Remirro pacified and unified the Romagna, winning great credit for himself. Then the duke decided that there was no need for this excessive authority, which might grow intolerable, and he established in the centre of the province a civil tribunal, under an eminent president,[3] on which every city had its own representative. Knowing also that the severities of the past had earned him a certain amount of hatred, to purge the minds of the people and to win them over completely he determined to show that if cruelties had been inflicted they were not his doing but prompted by the harsh nature of his minister. This gave Cesare a pretext; then, one morning, Remirro's body was found cut in two pieces on the piazza at Cesena, with a block of wood and a bloody knife beside it. The brutality of this spectacle kept the people of the Romagna at once appeased and stupefied.

But let us go back to where we were before that digression. The duke found himself in a position of considerable power and, in part, safe against immediate threats, through possessing his own troops and having largely destroyed the forces of those who were near enough to do him harm. Then, wanting to expand further, he still had to go carefully regarding France, because he knew this would not have been allowed by the king, who had belatedly realized his mistaken policy. So Cesare started to seek new alliances and to temporize with France when her troops were on the expedition towards Naples directed against the Spaniards who were besieging Gaeta. His intention was to secure Spanish support; and he would have had immediate success, if Alexander had lived.

Those were his plans regarding the immediate future. Beyond that, his chief cause for anxiety was that the next successor to the papacy might prove unfriendly and might endeavour to take back what Alexander had given him. He sought to guard against this eventuality in four ways: by destroying all the families of the rulers he had despoiled, thus depriving the pope of the opportunity of using them against him; second, by winning over all the patricians in Rome, as I mentioned before, in order to hold the pope in check; third, by controlling the College of Cardinals as far as he could; fourth, by acquiring so much power himself before Alexander died that he could on his own withstand an initial attack. Of these four, he had, on the death of Alexander, accomplished three; and he had almost accomplished the fourth. He killed as many of the rulers he had despoiled as he could reach, and very few escaped; he had won over the Roman patricians, and he had a very large following in the College. As for extending his power, he had aimed at becoming the ruler of Tuscany. Perugia and Piombino he already possessed, Pisa was under his protection. And as soon as he need have no concern over France (he no longer had to, the French having already lost the kingdom of Naples to the Spaniards, with the result that both sides sought to buy his friendship) he would have pounced on Pisa. That done, Lucca and Siena would have surrendered at once, partly from spite towards the Florentines, and partly through fear; and the Florentines were at his mercy. Had he succeeded in all this (as he would have succeeded in the year that Alexander died) he would have acquired such strength and prestige that he would have been able to stand alone and been dependent no longer on the fortune and strength of others but on his own power and prowess. But Alexander died five years from the time Cesare took up the sword. He left him with his state in the Romagna consolidated but with everything else in the air, between two extremely powerful and hostile armies, and mortally ill. The duke was a man of such ferocity and prowess, and he understood so well that men must be either won over or destroyed, and the foundations he laid in so short a time were so sound, that, had those armies not been bearing down on him, or had he been in good health, he would have overcome every difficulty. The strength of the foundations he laid is evident:

because the Romagna waited for him for over a month; in Rome, even when he was more dead than alive, he was unmolested, and although the Baglioni, the Vitelli, and the Orsini entered the city they roused no one against him; if he could not make whom he wanted pope, he was at least able to keep the papacy from going to one he did not want. If, when Alexander died, he had been well himself, everything would have been easy for him. And he himself said to me, the day Julius II was elected,[4] that he had thought of everything that could happen when his father died, and found a remedy for everything except that he never thought that when he did so he himself would also be at the point of death.

So having summed up all that the duke did, I cannot possibly censure him. Rather, I think I have been right in putting him forward as an example for all those who have acquired power through good fortune and the arms of others. He was a man of great courage and high intentions, and he could not have conducted himself other than the way he did; his plans were frustrated only because Alexander's life was cut short and because of his own sickness.[5] So a new prince cannot find more recent examples than those set by the duke, if he thinks it necessary to secure himself against his enemies, win friends, conquer either by force or by stratagem, make himself both loved and feared by his subjects, followed and respected by his soldiers, if he determines to destroy those who can and will injure him, to reform ancient institutions, be severe yet loved, magnanimous and generous, and if he decides to destroy disloyal troops and create a new standing army, maintaining such relations with kings and princes that they have either to help him graciously or go carefully in doing him harm. The duke deserves censure only regarding the election of Pope Julius, where he made a bad choice. As I said, not being able to get a pope to his liking he could have kept the papacy from going to one who was not; and he should never have allowed the election of one of those cardinals he had injured, or one who would have cause to fear him. Men do you harm either because they fear you or because they hate you. Those to whom Cesare himself had done harm were, among others, San Pietro ad Vincula, Colonna, San Giorgio, Ascanio.[6] All the others, were they to be elected, had cause to fear him, except for Rouen[7] and the Spaniards. The Spaniards in the College were Cesare's countrymen, and under an obligation to him; Rouen was powerful in his own right, having the backing of the kingdom of France. The duke's aim, first and foremost, should have been to get a Spaniard elected pope and, failing that, to let it be Rouen, not San Pietro ad Vincula. Whoever believes that with great men new services wipe out old injuries deceives himself. So the duke's choice was a mistaken one; and it was the cause of his ultimate ruin.

VIII. *Those who come to power by crime*

As there are also two ways of becoming a prince which cannot altogether be attributed either to fortune or to prowess, I do not think I ought to leave them out, even though one of them can be dealt with at greater length under the heading of republics. The two I have in mind are when a man becomes prince by some criminal and nefarious method, and when a private citizen becomes prince of his native city with the approval of his fellow citizens. In dealing with the first method, I shall give two examples, one from the ancient world, one from the modern, without otherwise discussing the rights and wrongs of this subject, because I imagine that these examples are enough for anyone who had to follow them.

Agathocles, the Sicilian, not only from the status of a private citizen but from the lowest, most abject condition of life, rose to become king of Syracuse. At every stage of his career this man, the son of a potter, behaved like a criminal; none the less he accompanied his crimes with so much audacity and physical courage that when he joined the militia he rose through the ranks to become praetor of Syracuse. After he had been appointed to this position, he determined to make himself prince and to possess by force and without obligation to others what had been voluntarily conceded to him. He reached an understanding about this ambition of his with Hamilcar the Carthaginian, who was campaigning with his armies in Sicily. Then one morning he assembled the people and Senate of Syracuse, as if he meant to raise matters which affected the republic; and at a prearranged signal he had all the senators, along with the richest citizens, killed by his soldiers; and when they were dead he seized and held the government of that city, without encountering any other internal opposition. Although he was twice routed and finally besieged by the Carthaginians, not only did he successfully defend the city, but, leaving some of his troops to defend it, he invaded Africa with the rest, and in a short time lifted the siege and reduced the Carthaginians to severe straits. They were compelled to make a pact with him, contenting themselves with the possession of Africa and leaving Sicily to Agathocles. So whoever studies that man's actions and life will discover little or nothing that can be attributed to fortune, inasmuch as not by anyone's favour he rose through the ranks of the militia, as I said, and his progress was attended by countless difficulties and dangers; that was how he won his principality, and he maintained his position with many audacious and dangerous enterprises. Yet it cannot be called prowess to kill fellow-citizens, to betray friends, to be treacherous, pitiless, irreligious. These ways can win a prince power but not glory. One can draw attention to the prowess of Agathocles in confronting and surviving danger, and his courageous spirit in enduring and overcoming adversity, and it appears that he should not be judged inferior to any eminent commander; none the less, his brutal cruelty and inhumanity, his countless crimes, forbid his being honoured among eminent men. One cannot attribute to fortune or prowess what was accomplished by him without the help of either.

In our own time, during the pontificate of Alexander VI, there was Oliverotto of Fermo. Years before, he had been left fatherless as a small boy and was brought up by a maternal uncle called Giovanni Fogliani. In his early youth he was sent to serve as a soldier under

Paulo Vitelli[1] so that he could win high command after being trained by him. When Paulo died, Oliverotto soldiered under Vitellozzo, his brother; and in a very short time, as he was intelligent, and a man of courage and audacity, he became Vitellozzo's chief commander. But he thought it was servile to take orders from others, and so he determined that, with the help of some citizens of Fermo to whom the enslavement of their native city was more attractive than its liberty, and with the favour and help of the Vitellozzo, he would seize Fermo for himself. He wrote to Giovanni Fogliani saying that, having been many years away from home he wanted to come and see him and his city and to make some investigation into his own estate. He had worked for nothing else except honour, he went on, and in order that his fellow citizens might see that he had not spent his time in vain, he wanted to come honourably, with a mounted escort of a hundred companions and servants. He begged Giovanni to arrange a reception which would bring honour to Giovanni as well as to himself, as he was Giovanni's foster child. Giovanni failed in no duty of hospitality towards his nephew. He had him honourably welcomed by the citizens of Fermo and lodged him in his own mansion. There, after a few days had passed during which he waited in order to complete the secret arrangements for his future crime, Oliverotto prepared a formal banquet[2] to which he invited Giovanni Fogliani and the leading citizens of Fermo. After they had finished eating and all the other entertainment usual at such banquets was done with, Oliverotto artfully started to touch on subjects of grave importance, talking of the greatness of Pope Alexander and of Cesare his son, and of their enterprises. When Giovanni and the others began to discuss these subjects in turn, he got to his feet all of a sudden, saying that these were things to be spoken of somewhere more private, and he withdrew to another room, followed by Giovanni and all the other citizens. And no sooner were they seated than soldiers appeared from hidden recesses, and killed Giovanni and all the others. After this slaughter, Oliverotto mounted his horse, rode through the town, and laid siege to the palace of the governing council; consequently they were frightened into obeying him and into setting up a government of which he made himself the prince. And having put to death all who, because they would resent his rule, might injure him, he strengthened his position by founding new civil and military institutions. In this way, in the space of the year that he held the principality, he not only established himself in the city of Fermo but also made himself formidable to all the neighbouring states. His overthrow would have proved as difficult as that of Agathocles, if he had not let himself be tricked by Cesare Borgia when, at Sinigaglia, as was recounted above, Cesare trapped the Orsini and Vitellozzo Vitelli. Oliverotto was also trapped there, and a year after committing parricide he, along with Vitellozzo, the teacher as regards both his prowess and his crimes, was strangled.

One might well wonder how it as that Agathocles (and others like him) after countless treacheries and cruelties, could live securely in his own country and hold foreign enemies at bay, with never a conspiracy against him by his countrymen, inasmuch as many others, because of their cruel behaviour, have not been able to maintain their rule even in peaceful times, let alone in the uncertain times of war. I believe that here it is a question of cruelty used well or badly. We can say that cruelty is used well (if it is permissible to talk in this way of what is evil) when it is employed once for all, and one's safety depends on it, and then it is not persisted in but as far as possible turned to the good of one's subjects. Cruelty badly used is that which, although infrequent to start with, as time goes on, rather than disappearing, grows in intensity. Those who use the first method can, with God and with men, somewhat enhance their position, as did Agathocles; the others cannot possibly stay in power.

So it should be noted that when he seizes a state the new ruler must determine all the injuries that he will need to inflict. He must inflict them once for all, and not have to renew them every day, and in that way he will be able to set men's minds at rest and win them over to him when he confers benefits. Whoever acts otherwise, either through timidity or misjudgement, is always forced to have the knife ready in his hand and he can never depend on his subjects because they, suffering fresh and continuous violence, can never feel secure with regard to him. Violence must be inflicted once for all; people will then forget what it tastes like and so be less resentful. Benefits must be conferred gradually; and in that way they will taste better. Above all, a prince must live with his subjects in such a way that no development, either favourable or adverse, makes him vary his conduct. For, when adversity brings the need for it, there is no time to inflict harm; and the favours he may confer are profitless, because they are seen as being forced, and so they earn no thanks.

IX. *The constitutional principality*

But now we come to the other case, where a private citizen becomes the ruler of his country neither by crime nor by any other outrageous act of violence but by the favour of his fellow citizens (and this we can call a constitutional principality, to become the ruler of which one needs neither prowess alone nor fortune, but rather a lucky astuteness). I say that one becomes a prince in this case with the favour of the people or of the nobles.[1] These two different dispositions are found in every city; and the people are everywhere anxious not to be dominated or oppressed by the nobles, and the nobles are out to dominate and oppress the people. These opposed ambitions bring about one of three results: a principality, a free city, or anarchy.

A principality is created either by the people or by the nobles, according to whether the one or the other of these two classes is given the opportunity. What happens is that when the nobles see they cannot withstand the people, they start to increase the standing of one of their own numbers, and they make him prince in order to be able to achieve their own ends under his cloak. The people in the same way, when they see they cannot withstand the nobles, increase the standing of one of themselves and make him prince in

31

order to be protected by his authority. A man who becomes prince with the help of the nobles finds it more difficult to maintain his position than one who does so with the help of the people. As prince, he finds himself surrounded by many who believe they are his equals, and because of that he cannot command or manage them the way he wants. A man who becomes prince by favour of the people finds himself standing alone, and he has near him either no one or very few not prepared to take orders. In addition, it is impossible to satisfy the nobles honourably, without doing violence to the interests of others; but this can be done as far as the people are concerned. The people are more honest in their intentions than the nobles are, because the latter want to oppress the people, whereas they want only not to be oppressed. Moreover, a prince can never make himself safe against a hostile people: there are too many of them. He can make himself safe against the nobles, who are few. The worst that can happen to a prince when the people are hostile is for him to be deserted; but from the nobles, if hostile, he has to fear not only desertion but even active opposition. The nobles have more foresight and are more astute, they always act in time to safeguard their interests, and they take sides with the one whom they expect to win. Again, a prince must always live with the same people, but he can well do without the nobles, since he can make and unmake them every day, increasing and lowering their standing at will.

To clarify the discussion further, I say that there are two main considerations to be remembered in regard to the nobles: either they conduct themselves in such a way that they come to depend entirely on your fortunes, or they do not. Those who become dependent, and are not rapacious, must be honoured and loved; those who remain independent of you do so for two different reasons. They may do so because they are pusillanimous and naturally lacking in spirit; if so you should make use of them, especially those who are capable of giving sensible advice, since they will respect you when you are doing well, and you will have nothing to fear from them in times of adversity. But when they deliberately and for reasons of ambition remain independent of you, it is a sign that they are more concerned about themselves than about you. Against nobles such as these, a prince must safeguard himself, fearing them as if they were his declared enemies, because in times of adversity they will always help to ruin him.

A man who is made a prince by the favour of the people must work to retain their friendship; and this is easy for him because the people ask only not to be oppressed. But a man who has become prince against the will of the people and by the favour of the nobles should, before anything else, try to win the people over; this too is easy if he takes them under his protection. When men receive favours from someone they expected to do them ill, they are under a greater obligation to their benefactor; just so the people can in an instant become more amicably disposed towards the prince than if he had seized power by their favour. And there are many ways in which a prince can win them over. These vary according to circumstances, so no definite rule can be given and I shall not deal with them here. I shall only conclude that it is necessary for a prince to have the friendship of the people; otherwise he has no remedy in times of adversity.

Nabis, prince of the Spartans, withstood the whole of Greece and a triumphant Roman army, and successfully defended his country and his own authority against them.[2] All he had to do, when danger threatened, was to take steps against a few of his subjects; but this would not have been enough had the people been hostile to him. Let no one contradict this opinion of mine with that trite proverb, that he who builds on the people builds on mud. That may be so when a private citizen bases his power on the people and takes it for granted that the people will rescue him if he is in danger from enemies or from the magistrates. (In this case, he could often find he had made a mistake, as happened with the Gracchi in Rome and messer Giorgio Scali in Florence.) But if it is a prince who builds his power on the people, one who can command and is a man of courage, who does not despair in adversity, who does not fail to take precautions, and who wins general allegiance by his personal qualities and the institutions he establishes, he will never be let down by the people; and he will be found to have established his power securely.

Principalities usually come to grief when the transition is being made from limited power to absolutism. Princes taking this step rule either directly or through magistrates. In the latter case, their position is weaker and more dangerous, because they rely entirely on the will of those citizens who have been put in office; and these, especially in times of adversity, can very easily depose them either by positive action against them or by not obeying them. And when danger comes, the prince has no time to seize absolute authority, because the citizens and subjects, accustomed to taking orders from the magistrates, will not take them from him in a crisis. In disturbed times, also, men whom the prince can trust will be hard to find. So such a prince cannot rely on what he has experienced in times of tranquillity, when the citizens have need of his government. When things are quiet, everyone dances attendance, everyone makes promises, and everybody would die for him so long as death is far off. But in times of adversity, when the state has need of its citizens, there are few to be found. And this test of loyalty is all the more dangerous since it can be made only once. Therefore a wise prince must devise ways by which his citizens are always and in all circumstances dependent on him and on his authority; and then they will always be faithful to him.

x. *How the strength of every principality should be measured*

There is another consideration rightly to be borne in mind when inquiring into the characteristics of these principalities: and that is whether a prince has territory such that, in case of necessity, he can stand alone, or whether he must always have recourse to the

protection of others. To clarify this further, I say that, in my judgement, those princes can stand alone who have sufficient manpower
or money to assemble an army equal to an encounter with any
aggressor. In the same way, those princes must always have recourse
to others who cannot take the field against the enemy but are forced
to retreat behind walls and make their defence there. I have discussed
the first case already, and later on I shall say whatever occurs to me
on that subject. As for the second case, nothing can be said except
to advise such princes to strengthen and fortify their own towns and
not to worry about the country around. If a prince has fortified his
town well, and has arranged his government in the way I said (and
I shall say more about this), then an enemy will be very circumspect
in attacking him. Men always dislike enterprises where the snags
are evident, and it is obviously not easy to assault a town which
has been made into a bastion by a prince who is not hated by the
people.

The cities of Germany are wholly independent, they control only
limited territory, and obey the emperor only when they want to.
They fear neither him nor any neighbouring power, because they
are so fortified that everyone knows it would be a protracted, difficult
operation to reduce them. This is because they all have excellent
moats and walls; they have adequate artillery; they always lay in
public stocks of drink, food, and fuel to last a year. Over and above
this, every German city, making provision for the common people
without public loss, always keeps a year's supply of the wherewithal
for them to work at those trades which give them their livelihood
and are the sinews of the city itself. Military exercises always enjoy
a high standing, and they have many laws and institutions providing
for them.

Therefore a prince who has a well-fortified city and does not
make himself hated is secure against attack; yet even if there were
an attack, the besieger would have to abandon the enterprise with
ignominy, because the course of events is so variable that no one
can stay encamped with his army, in idleness, for a year. One might

well object: if the people have their possessions outside the walls of the city and see them being burned, they will not be able to contain themselves, and the length of the siege and their own self-interest will make them forget their duty to the prince. My answer to this is that a powerful, courageous prince will always be able to overcome all such difficulties, inspiring his subjects now with the hope that the ills they are enduring will not last long, now with fear of the enemy's cruelty, and taking effective measures against those who are too outspoken. In addition, the enemy will as a matter of course burn and pillage the countryside when he arrives, and he will do this at a time when the prince's subjects are still fired with enthusiasm for the defence, so the prince has all the less reason to worry, because by the time this enthusiasm has died down, the losses will already have been sustained and the damage done, and there will be no remedy for it. So the subjects will identify themselves even more with their prince, since now that their houses have already been burned and their lands pillaged in his defence they will consider that there is a strong bond of obligation on his part. The nature of man is such that people consider themselves put under an obligation as much by the benefits they confer as by those they receive. So, bearing all this in mind, it should not be difficult for a prudent prince to inspire his subjects with determination during a siege, so long as he has adequate provisions and means of defence.

XI. *Ecclesiastical principalities*

It now remains to discuss ecclesiastical principalities; and here the difficulties which have to be faced occur before the ruler is established, in that such principalities are won by prowess or by fortune but are kept without the help of either. They are maintained, in fact, by religious institutions, so powerfully mature that, no matter how the ruler acts and lives, they safeguard his government. Ecclesiastical princes alone possess states, and do not defend them; subjects, and do not govern them. And though their states are not defended they are not taken away from them; and their subjects, being without government, do not worry about it and neither can nor hope to overthrow it in favour of another. So these principalities alone are secure and happy. But as they are sustained by higher powers which the human mind cannot comprehend, I shall not argue about them; they are exalted and maintained by God, and so only a rash and presumptuous man would take it on himself to discuss them. None the less if anyone should ask me how it is that the Church has attained such great temporal power, inasmuch as, up to the time of Alexander,[1] the Italian potentates, and not only those who are called potentates but every baron and nobleman, even the pettiest, set it at naught, but now a king of France trembles before it, and it has been able to chase him out of Italy and ruin the Venetians, I should not think it superfluous to recall to some extent how it happened, even though the story is well known.

Before Charles, king of France, invaded Italy, that country was ruled by the pope, the Venetians, the king of Naples, the duke of Milan, and the Florentines. These powers necessarily had two main preoccupations: the one, that no armed foreign power should invade Italy; the other, that no one power among themselves should enlarge its dominion. Those who had especially to be watched were the pope and the Venetians. To hold the Venetians in check, an alliance of all the others was necessary, as was the case in the defence of Ferrara;[2] and to pin down the pope use was made of the Roman barons. As these were split into two factions, Orsini and Colonna, there was always scope for dissension between them; and while they remained armed before the very eyes of the pontiff they kept the papacy weak and insecure. Although sometimes a spirited pope, such as Sixtus, might come along, even such a man could never rid himself of this nuisance, for all his good fortune or statecraft. This was because of the brevity of Pope's reign. In the ten years that, on average, a pope ruled, he scarcely had time to crush one of the factions; and then, for example, if one pope had almost managed to destroy the Colonna, another came along hostile to the Orsini (so ensuring the resurgence of the Colonna), and yet did not have time enough to destroy the Orsini.

This meant that the temporal power of the pope was little respected in Italy. But then came the reign of Alexander VI, and he, more than any other pontiff who has ever lived, showed how much a pope could achieve with money and armed force. With Duke Valentino[3] as his instrument and the invasion by the French as his occasion, he brought about all those things I discussed above regarding the duke's activities. Although his aim was the aggrandizement of the duke, not of the Church, none the less what he did increased the greatness of the Church; and after his death, when the duke had been destroyed, the Church inherited the fruits of his labours. Then came Pope Julius. He found the Church already great, possessing the Romagna, with the Roman barons destroyed and, as a result of Alexander's vigour, the factions wiped out; and he also found ready to hand a means of accumulating wealth which had not been employed before Alexander. Julius not only continued but also improved on all these things. He planned to win Bologna for himself and to crush the Venetians and to chase the French out of Italy. He succeeded in all his enterprises, and earned all the more credit in as much as he did everything for the aggrandizement of the Church and not for that of any individual. He also kept the Orsini and Colonna factions in the same condition as he had found them. And although among these there were some leaders disposed to make trouble, two things held them in check: the one, the greatness of the Church, which overawed them; the other, their being without cardinals, who cause the tumults among them. These factions will never stay quiet when they have their own cardinals, because the latter stir up feuds, both in Rome and outside, and those barons are bound to come to the aid of their own side; and so conflicts and tumults among the barons are provoked by the ambition of the prelates. Now, His Holiness Pope Leo found the papacy in an extremely strong position; and it is our hope that, his immediate predecessors having established its greatness by force of arms, he, by his goodness and countless other virtues, will make it very great and revered.

XII. *Military organization and mercenary troops*

Having discussed in detail all the characteristics of the principalities I listed to start with, and having to some extent considered the reasons why they prosper or fail, and shown the methods often used to acquire and retain them, it now remains for me to discuss in general the various ways in which these principalities can organize themselves for attack or defence. We said above that a prince must build on sound foundations; otherwise he is bound to come to grief. The main foundations of every state, new states as well as ancient or composite ones, are good laws and good arms; and because you cannot have good laws without good arms, and where there are good arms, good laws inevitably follow, I shall not discuss laws but give my attention to arms.

Now, I say that the arms on which a prince bases the defence of his state are either his own, or mercenary, or auxiliary, or composite. Mercenaries and auxiliaries are useless and dangerous. If a prince bases the defence of his state on mercenaries he will never achieve stability or security. For mercenaries are disunited, thirsty for power, undisciplined, and disloyal; they are brave among their friends and cowards before the enemy; they have no fear of God, they do not keep faith with their fellow men; they avoid defeat just so long as they avoid battle; in peacetime you are despoiled by them, and in wartime by the enemy. The reason for all this is that there is no loyalty or inducement to keep them on the field apart from the little they are paid, and this is not enough to make them want to die for you. They are only too ready to serve in your army when you are not at war; but when war comes they either desert or disperse. I should have little need to labour this point, because the present ruin of Italy has been caused by nothing else but the reliance placed on mercenary troops for so many years. Although there were times when some made good use of them, and they appeared brave enough when matched against other mercenaries, when the foreigner invaded Italy they showed themselves for what they were. So it was that Charles, king of France, was able to conquer Italy with his billeting officers alone.[1] And he who said that the reasons for this were our own sins was telling the truth;[2] but they were those I have described, not the sins he thought. As they were sins committed by princes, they too have paid the penalty for them.

I want to show more clearly what unhappy results follow the use of mercenaries. Mercenary commanders are either skilled in warfare or they are not: if they are, you cannot trust them, because they are anxious to advance their own greatness, either by coercing you, their employer, or by coercing others against your own wishes. If, however, the commander is lacking in prowess, in the normal way he brings about your ruin. If anyone argues that this is true of any other armed force, mercenary or not, I reply that armed forces must be under the control of either a prince or a republic: a prince should assume personal command and captain his troops himself; a republic must appoint its own citizens, and when a commander so appointed turns out incompetent, should change him, and if he is competent, it should limit his authority by statute. Experience has shown that only princes and armed republics achieve solid success, and that mercenaries bring nothing but loss; and a republic which has its own citizen army is far less likely to be subjugated by one of its own citizens than a republic whose forces are not its own.

Rome and Sparta endured for many centuries, armed and free. The Swiss are strongly armed and completely free. The Carthaginians provide an example of reliance on mercenary arms in ancient times. They were very nearly subjugated by their mercenary troops, after the first war with the Romans was over, even though their own citizens held the positions of command. After the death of Epaminondas, the Thebans put Philip of Macedon in command of their army; and when he had won a victory he robbed them of their liberty. After the death of Duke Filippo, the Milanese hired Francesco Sforza to soldier for them against the Venetians; and when he had defeated the enemy at Caravaggio he joined forces with them in order to subjugate his employers, the Milanese themselves. Sforza, his father, after being hired by Queen Joanna of Naples, deserted her without warning and left her defenceless; so to save her kingdom she was compelled to throw herself on the mercy of the king of Aragon.[3] Admittedly, the Venetians and the Florentines have in the past used mercenary arms to extend their power, and their commanders have fought to defend them, without however seizing the state. But my comment on this is that here the Florentines happen to have been lucky. As for the good commanders likely to cause them anxiety, one has failed to achieve military success, one has been checked in his designs, another has directed his ambition elsewhere. Giovanni Acuto was the one who proved unsuccessful, and, as that was so, his loyalty could not be put to the test; but everyone will admit that if he had been successful in battle the Florentines would have been in his power. The Sforzas always had the Bracceschi against them, and they held each other in check. Francesco directed his ambition towards Lombardy, Braccio against the Church and the kingdom of Naples.

But let us have a look at what happened a little while ago. As their commander the Florentines appointed Paulo Vitelli, a very shrewd man who, starting modestly, achieved considerable standing. Had he taken Pisa the Florentines would undeniably have had to fall in with his wishes, because if he had gone over to their enemies they would have been powerless against him; and keeping him in their service meant that they had to obey him. If the expansion of Venice is considered, it will be seen that the Venetians won glory for themselves and remained secure when they made war with their own forces (this was before they started to campaign on the mainland); with their own patricians and citizen army they displayed the greatest prowess. But when they started to fight on the mainland they lost this prowess and fell in with the military traditions of Italy. When they first started to acquire territory on the mainland they did not have much to fear from their commanders, as their dominions were still very limited and their standing was considerable. But when they expanded, with Carmagnola as their commander, they tasted the error of their ways. They had seen the great prowess of which Carmagnola was capable, and under his leadership they had defeated the duke of Milan. Then they perceived that he was only lukewarm in his conduct of the war and they realized that he would win no more battles for them; but they could not afford to dismiss him, lest they lost what they had acquired. So, for safety's sake, they were forced to kill him. They then appointed as their commanders Bartolommeo da Bergamo, Ruberto da San Severino, the count of Pitigliano, and men such as these; and when they were in command the question was whether the Venetians could hold on to what they had rather than whether they could hope for new gains. Such was the position at Vailà where, in one day's engagement, they lost what it had taken them eight hundred years' exertion to conquer.[4] Mercenary armies bring only slow, belated, and feeble conquests, but sudden, startling defeat. Since these examples have brought me to Italy, which for so many years has been dominated by mercenary arms, I would like to discuss them more thoroughly. If their origins and development have been made clear, it will be easier to provide a remedy.

You must realize that as soon as in more recent times Italy started to repudiate the Empire, and the standing of the papacy became higher in the temporal sphere, the country split into several states. What happened was that in many of the big cities there were uprisings against the nobles who had formerly, with the backing of the emperor, held them in subjection; and the Church, in order to increase its temporal authority, supported these revolts. In many other cities one of the citizens became prince. So Italy came to be almost entirely under the control of the Church and some few republics, and then, as the priests and townsmen had no experience in military matters, they started to hire foreign troops. The first to win a standing for this kind of army was Alberigo da Conio, of Romagna. From his school came, among others, Braccio and Sforza, who in their time were the masters of Italy. Then there followed all those other mercenaries up to our own times. And the result of their prowess has been that Italy has been overrun by Charles, plundered by Louis, occupied by Ferdinand, and outraged by the Swiss. It has been the policy of these mercenaries first to detract from the military standing of infantry in order to increase that of their own troops. They did this because, as they were stateless men soldiering for money, leadership of a few infantry troops did not give them any standing, while they could not provide adequately for large numbers. So they had recourse to cavalry, and in this way they were honoured and adequately provided for, while needing only tolerable numbers. Things came to such a pass that in an army of twenty thousand soldiers there would be hardly two thousand infantry. Beyond this, they directed all their efforts to ridding themselves and their soldiers of any cause for fear or need of exertion; instead of fighting to the death in their scrimmages they took prisoners, without demanding ransom. They never attacked garrison towns by night; and if they were besieged they never made a sortie; they did not bother to fortify their camps with stockades or ditches; they never campaigned in winter. All these things were permissible under their military code, and this policy was followed by them so that, as I said, they might escape both exertion and danger: and as a result they have led Italy into slavery and ignominy.

XIII. *Auxiliary, composite, and native troops*

Auxiliaries, the other useless kind of troops, are involved when you call upon a powerful state to come to your defence and assistance. Pope Julius did this in the recent past, when, having seen the sad account given of themselves by his mercenaries in the Ferrara campaign, he turned to auxiliaries and arranged for Ferdinand of

Spain to assist him with his men and troops. In themselves, auxiliary forces can prove useful and reliable, but for the one who calls them in they are almost always a disaster. You are left in the lurch if they are defeated, and in their power if they are victorious. Although ancient history is full of examples, none the less I will be content with the fresh example provided by Pope Julius II. His course of action could not have been more ill-considered when, wanting to take Ferrara, he threw himself into the hands of a foreigner. But such was his good fortune that something else happened which prevented his reaping what he had sown: after his auxiliaries were routed at Ravenna, the Swiss arrived on the scene and drove the victors off, so that to everyone's surprise, including his own, Julius escaped being at the mercy of the enemy (as they had fled) or being in the power of his own auxiliaries (as he had not conquered with their arms).[1] The Florentines, being completely without forces, hired ten thousand Frenchmen to reduce Pisa; because of which decision they incurred more dangers than at any time during their troubles. The emperor of Constantinople, to withstand his neighbours, sent into Greece ten thousand Turks who, when the war was over, refused to leave; and this was how the infidels started to enslave Greece.[2] So anyone who does not want military success should have recourse to this kind of force, because it is far more dangerous than a mercenary army. Auxiliaries are fatal; they constitute a united army, wholly obedient to the orders of someone else; but mercenaries, having conquered, need more time and opportunity to harm you, for they are not a compact force and you have raised and paid them yourself. Mercenaries, also, are led by someone you appoint, and he cannot immediately assume sufficient authority to be able to do you harm. To sum up, cowardice is the danger with mercenaries, and valour with auxiliaries.

Wise princes, therefore, have always shunned auxiliaries and made use of their own forces. They have preferred to lose battles with their own forces than win them with others, in the belief that no true victory is possible with alien arms. Now, I shall never hesitate to cite Cesare Borgia and his conduct as an example. The duke used auxiliaries in his invasion of the Romagna, going there at the head of French troops. With those, he took Imola and Forlì. But then he decided that they were unsafe, and he turned to mercenaries in the belief that less risk was involved, hiring the Orsini and the Vitelli. In making use of these, he found them to be suspect, disloyal, and dangerous; so he got rid of them and raised his own forces. And one can easily see the different between these forces by considering the difference between the standing of the duke when he had only the French, when he had the Orsini and the Vitelli, and when he relied only on his own forces and himself. He grew in stature at each stage; and he was held in real respect only when everyone saw that he was absolute master of his armies.

I did not want to depart from recent, Italian examples, yet I do not want to ignore Hiero of Syracuse, one of those I mentioned before. As I said then, when the Syracusans had given him command of their armies he immediately realized that the mercenaries were useless; they were hired troops organized like our Italian mercenaries. It seemed to him impossible either to keep them or to disband them, so he had them all cut to pieces. And then he made war with his own, not with alien, soldiers. I would also like to recall to mind an allegory from the Old Testament, which is relevant to my argument. David offered Saul to go and fight Goliath, the Philistine champion, and Saul, to inspire him with courage, gave him his own weapons and armour. Having tried these on, David rejected them, saying that he would be unable to fight well with them and therefore he wanted to face the enemy with his sling and his knife. In short, armour belonging to someone else either drops off you or weighs you down or is too tight. When Charles VII, the father of King Louis XI, had by good fortune and prowess liberated France from the English, he realized the need to have his own armed forces, and set up the militia composed of mounted troops and infantry.[3] Subsequently, his son King Louis abolished the ordinance governing the infantry and started to hire Swiss soldiers; and this mistake, followed by others, has as we can now see been the cause of the dangers threatening that kingdom.[4] The increased standing allowed the Swiss has demoralized the rest of the army; the infantry have been abolished altogether, and the mounted troops have been made dependent on foreign troops, because being accustomed to take the field along with the Swiss they have come to believe that without them they cannot win a battle. Because of this, the French are no match for the Swiss, and without Swiss help feel no match for anyone else. So France has made use of a mixed force, partly mercenary and partly citizen: this combination is far better than a purely auxiliary or purely mercenary force, and far inferior to a citizen army. The example of France should be enough, because that kingdom would be unbeatable if what Charles had instituted had been developed or maintained. But men are so imprudent that they take up a diet which, as it tastes good to start with, they do not realize is poisonous, a point I made before when talking about wasting fevers.

The prince who does not detect evils the moment they appear is lacking in true wisdom; but few rulers have the ability to do so. If we consider what was the start of the downfall of the Roman empire, it will be found that it was simply when the Goths started to be hired as mercenaries. To that small beginning can be traced the enervation of the forces of the Roman empire. And the Goths inherited the prowess which the Romans lost.

I conclude, therefore, that unless it commands its own arms no principality is secure; rather, it is dependent on fortune, since there is no valour and no loyalty to defend it when adversity comes. Wise men have always held and believed: '*quod nihil sit tam infirmum aut instabile quam fama potentiae non sua vi nixa*'.[5] One's own forces are composed of an army of one's subjects or an army of citizens or dependants; all other forces are either mercenaries or auxiliaries. It is easy to discover how to organize one's own forces if one studies the precedents set by the four rulers I named above, and if one understands how Philip, the father of Alexander the Great, and many other republics and princes, have armed and organized themselves: I willingly defer to the wisdom of what they instituted.

XIV. *How a prince should organize his militia*

A prince, therefore, must have no other object or thought, nor acquire skill in anything, except war, its organization, and its discipline. The art of war is all that is expected of a ruler; and it is so useful that besides enabling hereditary princes to maintain their rule it frequently enables ordinary citizens to become rulers. On the other hand, we find that princes who have thought more of their pleasures than of arms have lost their states. The first way to lose your state is to neglect the art of war; the first way to win a state is to be skilled in the art of war.

Francesco Sforza, because he was armed, from being an ordinary citizen rose to be duke of Milan; his sons, because they fled the hardships involved, sank to being ordinary citizens after being dukes. You are bound to meet misfortune if you are unarmed because, among other reasons, people despise you, and this, as I shall say later on, is one of the infamies a prince should be on his guard against. There is simply no comparison between a man who is armed and one who is not. It is unreasonable to expect that an armed man should obey one who is unarmed, or that an unarmed man should remain safe and secure when his servants are armed. In the latter case, there will be suspicion on the one hand and contempt on the other, making cooperation impossible. So a prince who does not understand warfare, as well as the other misfortunes he invites, cannot be respected by his soldiers or place any trust in them.

So he must never let his thoughts stray from military exercises, which he must pursue more vigorously in peace than in war. These exercises can be both physical and mental. As for the first, besides keeping his men well organized and trained, he must always be out hunting, so accustoming his body to hardships and also learning some practical geography: how the mountains slope, how the valleys open, how the plains spread out. He must study rivers and marshes; and in all this he should take great pains. Such knowledge is useful in two ways: first, if he obtains a clear understanding of local geography he will have a better understanding of how to organize his defence; and in addition his knowledge of and acquaintance with local conditions will make it easy for him to grasp the features of any new locality with which he may need to familiarize himself. For example, the hills and valleys, the plains, the rivers, and the marshes of Tuscany have certain features in common with those of other provinces; so with a knowledge of the geography of one particular province one can easily acquire knowledge of the geography of others. The prince who lacks this knowledge also lacks the first qualification of a good commander. This kind of ability teaches him how to locate the enemy, where to take up quarters, how to lead his army on the march and draw it up for battle, and lay siege to a town to the best advantage.

Philopoemen, the leader of the Achaeans, has been praised by the historians for, among other things, having never in peacetime thought of anything else except military strategy. When he was in the country with his friends, he would often stop and invite a discussion: If the enemy were on top of that hill, and we were down here with our army, which of us would have the advantage? How would one engage them without breaking ranks? If we wanted to retreat, how would we have to set about it? If they retreated, how would we best pursue them?

And, as they went along, he expounded to his friends all the contingencies that can befall an army; he heard their opinion, gave his own, and corroborated it with reasons. As a result, because of these continuous speculations, when he was leading his armies he knew how to cope with all and every emergency.

As for intellectual training, the prince must read history, studying the actions of eminent men to see how they conducted themselves during war and to discover the reasons for their victories or their defeats, so that he can avoid the latter and imitate the former. Above all, he must read history so that he can do what eminent men have done before him: taken as their model some historical figure who has been praised and honoured; and always kept his deeds and actions before them. In this way, it is said, Alexander the Great imitated Achilles; Caesar imitated Alexander; and Scipio, Cyrus. And anyone who reads the life of Cyrus, written by Xenophon, will then see how much of the glory won by Scipio can be attributed to his emulation of Cyrus, and how much, in his chastity, courtesy, humanity, and generosity, Scipio conformed to the picture which Xenophon drew of Cyrus.

A wise prince must observe these rules; he must never take things easy in times of peace, but rather use the latter assiduously, in order to be able to reap the profit in times of adversity. Then, when his fortunes change, he will be found ready to resist adversity.

xv. *The things for which men, and especially princes, are praised or blamed*

It now remains for us to see how a prince must regulate his conduct towards his subjects or his allies.[1] I know that this has often been written about before, and so I hope it will not be thought presumptuous for me to do so, as, especially in discussing this subject, I draw up an original set of rules. But since my intention is to say something that will prove of practical use to the inquirer, I have thought it proper to represent things as they are in a real truth, rather than as they are imagined. Many have dreamed up republics and principalities which have never in truth been known to exist; the gulf between how one should live and how one does live is so wide that a man who neglects what is actually done for what should be done moves towards self-destruction rather than self-preservation. The fact is that a man who wants to act virtuously in every way necessarily

49

comes to grief among so many who are not virtuous. Therefore if a prince wants to maintain his rule he must be prepared not to be virtuous, and to make use of this or not according to need.

So leaving aside imaginary things about a prince, and referring only to those which truly exist, I say that whenever men are discussed and especially princes (who are more exposed to view), they are judged for various qualities which earn them either praise or condemnation. Some, for example, are held to be generous, and others miserly (I use the Tuscan word rather than the word avaricious: we also call a man who is mean with what he possesses, miserly, whereas avaricious applies also to a man who wants to plunder others).[2] Some are held to be benefactors, others are called grasping; some cruel, some compassionate; one man faithless, another faithful; one man effeminate and cowardly, another fierce and courageous; one man courteous, another proud; one man lascivious, another chaste; one guileless, another crafty; one stubborn, another flexible; one grave, another frivolous; one religious, another sceptical; and so forth. I know everyone will agree that it would be most laudable if a prince possessed all the qualities deemed to be good among those I have enumerated. But, because of conditions in the world, princes cannot have those qualities, or observe them completely. So a prince has of necessity to be so prudent that he knows how to escape the evil reputation attached to those vices which could lose him his state, and how to avoid those vices which are not so dangerous, if he possibly can; but, if he cannot, he need not worry so much about the latter. And then, he must not flinch from being blamed for vices which are necessary for safeguarding the state. This is because, taking everything into account, he will find that some of the things that appear to be virtues will, if he practises them, ruin him, and some of the things that appear to be vices will bring him security and prosperity.

XVI. *Generosity and parsimony*

So, starting with the first of the qualities I enumerated above, I say it would be splendid if one had a reputation for generosity; none the less if you do in fact earn a reputation for generosity you will come to grief. This is because if your generosity is good and sincere it may pass unnoticed and it will not save you from being reproached for its opposite. If you want to sustain a reputation for generosity, therefore, you have to be ostentatiously lavish; and a prince acting in that fashion will soon squander all his resources, only to be forced in the end, if he wants to maintain his reputation, to lay excessive burdens on the people, to impose extortionate taxes, and to do everything else he can to raise money. This will start to make his subjects hate him, and, since he will have impoverished himself, he will be generally despised. As a result, because of this generosity of his, having injured many and rewarded few, he will be vulnerable to the first minor setback, and the first real danger he encounters will bring him to grief. When he realizes this and tries to retrace his path he will immediately be reputed a miser.

So because a prince cannot practise the virtue of generosity in such a way that he is noted for it, except to his cost, he should if he is prudent not mind being called a miser. In time he will be recognized as being essentially a generous man, seeing that because of his parsimony his existing revenues are enough for him, he can defend himself against an aggressor, and he can embark on campaigns without burdening the people. So he proves himself generous to all those from whom he takes nothing, and they are innumerable, and miserly towards all those to whom he gives nothing, and they are few. In our own times great things have been accomplished only by those who have been held miserly, and the others have met disaster. Pope Julius II made use of a reputation for generosity to win the papacy but subsequently he made no effort to maintain this reputation, because he wanted to be able to finance his wars. The present king of France has been able to wage so many wars without taxing his subjects excessively only because his long-standing parsimony enabled him to meet the additional expenses involved. Were the present king of Spain[1] renowned for his generosity he would not have started and successfully concluded so many enterprises.

So a prince must think little of it, if he incurs the name of miser, so as not to rob his subjects, to be able to defend himself, not to become poor and despicable, not to be forced to grow rapacious. Miserliness is one of those vices which sustain his rule. Someone may object: Caesar came to power by virtue of his generosity, and many others, because they practised and were known for their generosity, have risen to the very highest positions. My answer to this is as follows. Either you are already a prince, or you are on the way to becoming one. In the first case, your generosity will be to your cost; in the second, it is certainly necessary to have a reputation for generosity. Caesar was one of those who wanted to establish his own rule over Rome; but if, after he had established it, he had remained alive and not moderated his expenditure he would have fallen from power.

Again, someone may retort: there have been many princes who have won great successes with their armies, and who have had the reputation of being extremely generous. My reply to this is: the prince gives away what is his own or his subjects', or else what belongs to others. In the first case he should be frugal; in the second, he should indulge his generosity to the full. The prince who campaigns with his armies, who lives by pillaging, sacking, and extortion, disposes of what belongs to aliens; and he must be open-handed, otherwise the soldiers would refuse to follow him. And you can be more liberal with what does not belong to you or your subjects, as Caesar, Cyrus, and Alexander were. Giving away what belongs to strangers in no way affects your standing at home; rather it increases it. You hurt yourself only when you give away what is your own. There is nothing so self-defeating as generosity: in the act of practising it, you lose the ability to do so, and you become either poor and despised or, seeking to escape poverty, rapacious and hated. A prince must try to avoid, above all else, being despised and hated; and generosity results in your being both. Therefore it is wiser to incur the reputation of being a miser, which brings forth ignominy but not hatred, than to be forced by seeking a name for generosity to incur a reputation for rapacity, which brings you hatred as well as ignominy.

XVII Cruelty and compassion; and whether it is better to be loved than feared, or the reverse

Taking others of the qualities I enumerated above, I say that a prince must want to have a reputation for compassion rather than for cruelty: none the less, he must be careful that he does not make bad use of compassion. Cesare Borgia was accounted cruel; nevertheless, this cruelty of his reformed the Romagna, brought it unity, and restored order and obedience. On reflection, it will be seen that there was more compassion in Cesare than in the Florentine people, who, to escape being called cruel, allowed Pistoia to be devastated.[1] So a prince must not worry if he incurs reproach for his cruelty so long as he keeps his subjects united and loyal. By making an example or two he will prove more compassionate than those who, being too compassionate, allow disorders which lead to murder and rapine. These nearly always harm the whole community, whereas executions ordered by a prince only affect individuals. A new prince, of all rulers, finds it impossible to avoid a reputation for cruelty, because of the abundant dangers inherent in a newly won state. Vergil, through the mouth of Dido, says:

> *Res dura, et regni novitas me talia cogunt*
> *Moliri, et late fines custode tueri.*[2]

None the less, a prince must be slow to believe allegations and to take action, and must watch that he does not come to be afraid of his own shadow; his behaviour must be tempered by humanity and prudence so that over-confidence does not make him rash or excessive distrust make him unbearable.

From this arises the following question: whether it is better to be loved than feared, or the reverse. The answer is that one would like to be both the one and the other; but because it is difficult to combine them, it is far better to be feared than loved if you cannot be both. One can make this generalization about men: they are ungrateful, fickle, liars, and deceivers, they shun danger and are greedy for profit; while you treat them well, they are yours. They would shed their blood for you, risk their property, their lives, their sons, so long, as I said above, as danger is remote; but when you are in danger they turn away. Any prince who has come to depend entirely on promises and has taken no other precautions ensures his own ruin; friendship which is bought with money and not with greatness and nobility of mind is paid for, but it does not last and it yields nothing. Men worry less about doing an injury to one who makes himself loved than to one who makes himself feared. For love is secured by a bond of gratitude which men, wretched creatures that they are, break when it is to their advantage to do so; but fear is strengthened by a dread of punishment which is always effective.

The prince must none the less make himself feared in such a way that, if he is not loved, at least he escapes being hated. For fear is quite compatible with an absence of hatred; and the prince can always avoid hatred if he abstains from the property of his subjects and citizens and from their women. If, even so, it proves necessary to execute someone, this is to be done only when there is proper justification and manifest reason for it. But above all a prince must abstain from the property of others; because men sooner forget the death of their father than the loss of their patrimony. It is always possible to find pretexts for confiscating someone's property; and a prince who starts to live by rapine always finds pretexts for seizing what belongs to others. On the other hand, pretexts for executing someone are harder to find and they are sooner gone.

However, when a prince is campaigning with his soldiers and is in command of a large army then he need not worry about having a reputation for cruelty; because, without such a reputation, no army was ever kept united and disciplined. Among the admirable achievements of Hannibal is included this: that although he led a huge army, made up of countless different races, on foreign campaigns, there was never any dissension, either among the troops themselves or against their leader, whether things were going well or badly. For this, his inhuman cruelty was wholly responsible. It was this, along with his countless other qualities, which made him feared and respected by his soldiers. If it had not been for his cruelty, his other qualities would not have been enough. The historians, having given little thought to this, on the one hand admire what Hannibal achieved, and on the other condemn what made his achievements possible.

That his other qualities would not have been enough by themselves can be proved by looking at Scipio, a man unique in his own time and through all recorded history. His armies mutinied against him in Spain, and the only reason for this was his excessive leniency, which allowed his soldiers more licence than was good for military discipline. Fabius Maximus reproached him for this in the Senate and called him a corrupter of the Roman legions. Again, when the Locrians were plundered by one of Scipio's officers, he neither gave them satisfaction nor punished his officer's insubordination; and this was all because of his being too lenient by nature.[3] By way of excuse for him some senators argued that many men were better at not making mistakes themselves than at correcting them in others. But in time Scipio's lenient nature would have spoilt his fame and glory had he continued to indulge it during his command; when he lived under orders from the Senate, however, this fatal characteristic of his was not only concealed but even brought him glory.

So, on this question of being loved or feared, I conclude that since some men love as they please but fear when the prince pleases, a wise prince should rely on what he controls, not on what he cannot control. He must only endeavour, as I said, to escape being hated.

XVIII. *How princes should honour their word*

Everyone realizes how praiseworthy it is for a prince to honour his word and to be straightforward rather than crafty in his dealings; none the less contemporary experience shows that princes who have achieved great things have been those who have given their word lightly, who have known how to trick men with their cunning, and who, in the end, have overcome those abiding by honest principles.

You must understand, therefore, that there are two ways of fighting: by law or by force. The first way is natural to men, and the second to beasts. But as the first way often proves inadequate one must needs have recourse to the second. So a prince must understand how to make a nice use of the beast and the man. The ancient writers taught princes about this by an allegory, when they described how Achilles and many other princes of the ancient world were sent to be brought up by Chiron, the centaur, so that he might train them his way. All the allegory means, in making the teacher half beast and half man, is that a prince must know how to act according to the nature of both, and that he cannot survive otherwise.

So, as a prince is forced to know how to act like a beast, he must learn from the fox and the lion; because the lion is defenceless against traps and a fox is defenceless against wolves. Therefore one must be a fox in order to recognize traps, and a lion to frighten off wolves. Those who simply act like lions are stupid. So it follows that a prudent ruler cannot, and must not, honour his word when it places him at a disadvantage and when the reasons for which he made his promise no longer exist. If all men were good, this precept would not be good; but because men are wretched creatures who would not keep their word to you, you need not keep your word to them.

And no prince ever lacked good excuses to colour his bad faith. One could give innumerable modern instances of this, showing how many pacts and promises have been made null and void by the bad faith of princes: those who have known best how to imitate the fox have come off best. But one must know how to colour one's actions and to be a great liar and deceiver. Men are so simple, and so much creatures of circumstance, that the deceiver will always find someone ready to be deceived.

There is one fresh example I do not want to omit. Alexander VI never did anything, or thought of anything, other than deceiving men; and he always found victims for his deceptions. There never was a man capable of such convincing asseverations, or so ready to swear to the truth of something, who would honour his word less. None the less his deceptions always had the result he intended, because he was a past master in the art.

A prince, therefore, need not necessarily have all the good qualities I mentioned above, but he should certainly appear to have them. I would even go so far as to say that if he has these qualities and always behaves accordingly he will find them harmful; if he only appears to have them they will render him service. He should appear to be compassionate, faithful to his word, kind, guileless, and devout. And indeed he should be so. But his disposition should be such that, if he needs to be the opposite, he knows how. You must realize this: that a prince, and especially a new prince, cannot observe all those things which give men a reputation for virtue, because in order to maintain his state he is often forced to act in defiance of good faith, of charity, of kindness, of religion. And so he should have a flexible disposition, varying as fortune and circumstances dictate. As I said above, he should not deviate from what is good, if that is possible, but he should know how to do evil, if that is necessary.

A prince, then, must be very careful not to say a word which does not seem inspired by the five qualities I mentioned earlier. To those seeing and hearing him, he should appear a man of compassion, a man of good faith, a man of integrity, a kind and a religious man.

And there is nothing so important as to seem to have this last quality. Men in general judge by their eyes rather than by their hands; because everyone is in a position to watch, few are in a position to come in close touch with you. Everyone sees what you appear to be, few experience what you really are. And those few dare not gainsay the many who are backed by the majesty of the state. In the actions of all men, and especially of princes, where there is no court of appeal, one judges by the result. So let a prince set about the task of conquering, and maintaining his state; his methods will always be judged honourable and will be universally praised. The common people are always impressed by appearances and results. In this context, there are only common people, and there is no leeway for the few when the many are firmly sustained. A certain contemporary ruler, whom it is better not to name, never preaches anything except peace and good faith;[1] and he is an enemy of both one and the other, and if he had ever honoured either of them he would have lost either his standing or his state many times over.

XIX. *The need to avoid contempt and hatred*

Now, having talked about the most important of the qualities enumerated above, I want to discuss the others briefly under this generalization: that the prince should, as I have already suggested, determine to avoid anything which will make him hated and despised. So long as he does so, he will have done what he should and he will run no risk whatsoever if he is reproached for the other vices I mentioned. He will be hated above all if, as I said, he is rapacious and aggressive with regard to the property and the women of his subjects. He must refrain from these. As long as he does not rob the great majority of their property or their honour, they remain content. He then has to contend only with the ambition of a few, and that can be dealt with easily and in a variety of ways. He will be despised if he has a reputation for being fickle, frivolous, effeminate, cowardly, irresolute; a prince should avoid this like the plague and strive to demonstrate in his actions grandeur, courage, sobriety, strength. When settling disputes between his subjects, he should ensure that his judgement is irrevocable; and he should be so regarded that no one ever dreams of trying to deceive or trick him.

The prince who succeeds in having himself thus regarded is highly esteemed; and against a man who is highly esteemed conspiracy is difficult, and open attack is difficult, provided he is recognized as a great man, who is respected by his subjects. There are two things a prince must fear: internal subversion from his subjects; and external aggression by foreign powers. Against the latter, his defence lies in being well armed and having good allies; and if he is well armed he will always have good allies. In addition, domestic affairs will always remain under control provided that relations with external powers are under control and if indeed they were not disturbed by a conspiracy. Even if there is disturbance abroad, if the prince has ordered his government and lived as I said, and if he does not capitulate, he will always repulse every onslaught, just as I said Nabis the Spartan did. Now, as far as his subjects are concerned, when there is no disturbance abroad the prince's chief fear must be a secret conspiracy. He can adequately guard against this if he avoids being hated or scorned and keeps the people satisfied: this, as I have said above at length, is crucial. One of the most powerful safeguards a prince can have against conspiracies is to avoid being hated by the populace. This is because the conspirator always thinks that by killing the prince he will satisfy the people; but if he thinks that he will outrage the people, he will never have the courage to go ahead with his enterprise, because there are countless obstacles in the path of a conspirator. As experience shows, there have been many conspiracies but few of them have achieved their end. This is because the conspirator needs others to help him, and those have to be men who, he believes, are disgruntled. But as soon as he reveals his mind to a man who is dissatisfied he gives him the means to get satisfaction, because by telling all he knows the latter can hope to obtain all he wants. Seeing the sure profit to be won by informing, and the highly dangerous and doubtful alternative, a man must be either a rare friend indeed or else an utterly relentless enemy of the prince to keep faith with you. To put it briefly, I say that on the side of the conspirator there is nothing except fear, envy, and the terrifying prospect of punishment; on the side of the prince there is the majesty of government, there are laws, the resources of his friends and of the state to protect him. Add to all these the goodwill of the people, and it is unthinkable that anyone should be so rash as to conspire. For whereas in the normal course of events a conspirator has cause for fear before he acts, in this case he has cause for fear afterwards as well, seeing that the people are hostile to him. He will have accomplished his crime, and, because the people are against him, he will have no place of refuge.

I could give countless illustrations of this; but I will content myself with just one, which happened in the time of our fathers. The Canneschi conspired against and killed messer Annibale Bentivogli, grandfather of the present Annibale, and prince of Bologna. There remained as his heir only messer Giovanni, who was still in swaddling clothes. Immediately this murder was perpetrated, the people rose up and killed all the Canneschi. They were inspired by the goodwill that existed for the House of Bentivoglio at that period. It was so great that, although there was no member of the family left in Bologna to take over the government on the death of Annibale, the citizens of Bologna, hearing that there was someone in Florence who was of the Bentivoglio family but had until then been thought to be the son of a smith, went there to find him. They entrusted him with the government of the city; and he ruled until Giovanni was old enough to assume the government himself.

I conclude, therefore, that when a prince has the goodwill of the people he must not worry about conspiracies; but when the people are hostile and regard him with hatred he must go in fear of everything and everyone. Well-organized states and wise princes have always taken great pains not to make the nobles despair, and to satisfy the people and keep them content; this is one of the most important tasks a prince must undertake.

Among kingdoms which are well organized and governed, in our own time, is that of France: it possesses countless valuable institutions, on which the king's freedom of action and security depend. The first of these is the parliament and its authority. For the lawgiver of the French kingdom, knowing the ambition and insolence of the powerful, judged it necessary that they should be restrained by having a bit in their mouths. On the other hand, he wanted to protect the masses, knowing how they feared, and therefore hated, the nobles. He did not want this to be the particular responsibility of the king, because he wished to save him from being reproached by the nobles for favouring the people and by the people for favouring the nobles. So he instituted an independent arbiter to crush the nobles and favour the weak, without bringing reproach on the king. There could be no better or more sensible institution, nor one more effective in ensuring the security of the king and the kingdom.

From this can be drawn another noteworthy consideration: that princes should delegate to others the enactment of unpopular measures and keep in their own hands the means of winning favours. Again, I conclude that a prince should value the nobles, but not make himself hated by the people.

Many who have studied the lives and deaths of certain Roman emperors may perhaps believe that they provide examples contradicting my opinion; some emperors who led consistently worthy lives, and showed strength of character, none the less fell from power, or were even done to death by their own men who conspired against them. As I wish to answer these objections, I shall discuss the characters of some of the emperors, showing that the reasons for their downfall are not different from those I have adduced. I shall submit for consideration examples which are well known to students of the period. I shall also restrict myself to all those emperors who came to power from Marcus the philosopher to Maximinus. These were: Marcus Aurelius, Commodus his son, Pertinax, Julian, Severus,

Caracalla his son, Macrinus, Heliogabalus, Alexander, and Maxi-minus.[1]

First, it is to be noted that whereas other princes have to contend only with the ambition of the nobles and the insolence of the people, the Roman emperors encountered a third difficulty: they had to contend with the cruelty and avarice of the soldiers. This was a hard task and it was responsible for the downfall of many, since it was difficult to satisfy both the soldiers and the populace. The latter, being peace-loving, liked unadventurous emperors, while the soldiers loved a warlike ruler, and one who was arrogant, cruel, and rapacious. They wanted him to treat the people accordingly, so that they could be paid more and could give vent to their own avarice and cruelty. As a result, those emperors who did not have the natural authority or the standing to hold both the soldiers and the populace in check always came to grief. Most of them, especially those who were new to government, when they recognized the difficulty of satisfying these two diverse elements, appeased the soldiers and did not worry about injuring the populace. This policy was necessary: princes cannot help arousing hatred in some quarters, so first they must strive not to be hated by all and every class of subject; and when this proves impossible, they should strive assiduously to escape the hatred of the most powerful classes. Therefore those emperors who, because they were new men, needed out of the ordinary support, were more ready to throw in their lot with the soldiers than with the people. None the less, this proved to be advantageous or not depending on whether the ruler knew how to maintain his standing with the troops. Now, for the reasons given above, it came about that Marcus Aurelius, Pertinax, and Alexander, who all lived unadventurously, who loved justice, hated cruelty, were kind and courteous, all, Marcus apart, had an unhappy end. Marcus alone was held during his life and after in high esteem, because he succeeded to the empire by hereditary right, and did not have to thank either the soldiers or the populace for it. Then, as he possessed many qualities which earned him great respect, all his life he succeeded in holding both of these in check and he was never hated or scorned. But Pertinax came to grief in the early stages of his administration; he was created emperor against the will of the soldiers, who had been used to living licentiously under Commodus and so could not tolerate the decency which Pertinax wished to impose on them. So the emperor made himself hated, and also, since he was an old man, scorned.

And here it should be noted that one can be hated just as much for good deeds as for evil ones; therefore, as I said above, a prince who wants to maintain his rule is often forced not to be good, because whenever that class of men on which you believe your continued rule depends is corrupt, whether it be the populace, or soldiers, or nobles, you have to satisfy it by adopting the same disposition; and then good deeds are your enemies. But let us come to Alexander. He was a man of such goodness that, among the other things for which he is given credit, it is said that during the fourteen years he reigned he never put anyone to death without trial. None the less, as he was thought effeminate, and a man who let himself be ruled by his mother, he came to be scorned, and the army conspired against him and killed him.

Discussing in contrast the characters of Commodus, Severus, Antonius Caracalla, and Maximinus, you will find them to have been extremely cruel and rapacious. To satisfy the soldiers, there was no kind of injury they did not inflict on the people; and all of them, except Severus, came to an unhappy end. Severus was a man of such prowess that, keeping the soldiers friendly, even though the people were oppressed by him, he reigned successfully to the end; this was because his prowess so impressed the soldiers and the people that the latter were in a certain manner left astonished and stupefied and the former stayed respectful and content.

Because what Severus did was remarkable and outstanding for a new prince, I want to show briefly how well he knew how to act the part of both a fox and a lion, whose natures, as I say above, must be imitated by a new prince. Knowing the indolence of the emperor

Julian, Severus persuaded the troops he commanded in Slavonia to march on Rome to avenge the death of Pertinax, who had been put to death by the Praetorian Guards. Under this pretext, without any indication that he aspired to the empire, he moved the army against Rome; and he arrived in Italy before it was known that he had set out. When he came, the Senate, out of fear, elected him emperor and put Julian to death. After this start, there remained two obstacles in the way of his becoming master of all the state: one was in Asia, where Pescennius Niger, commander of the Asiatic army, had had himself proclaimed emperor; the other was in the west, where Albinus also aspired to the empire. Judging it was dangerous to show himself hostile to both of them, Severus decided to attack Niger and to trick Albinus. He wrote to the latter saying that, having been elected emperor by the Senate, he wished to share the high rank with him; he sent him the title of Caesar and, through a resolution in the Senate, he made him co-emperor. Albinus took all these things at their face value. But once Severus had defeated Niger and put him to death, and had pacified the East, he returned to Rome and complained in the Senate that Albinus, not recognizing the favours he had received from him, had treacherously sought to kill him. Because of this, Severus added, it was necessary for him to go and punish such ingratitude. He then marched against him in France, and took from him his state and his life.

So whoever carefully studies what this man did will find that he had the qualities of a ferocious lion and a very cunning fox, and that he was feared and respected by everyone, yet not hated by the troops. And it will not be thought anything to marvel at if Severus, an upstart, proved himself able to maintain such great power; because his tremendous prestige always protected him from the hatred which his plundering had inspired in the people. Now Antoninus Caracalla, his son, was also a man of splendid qualities which astonished the people and endeared him to the soldiers; he was a military man, capable of any exertion, and he scorned softness of any kind, at the table or elsewhere. This won him the devotion of the troops. None the less, his ferocity and cruelty were so great and unparalleled (after countless individual murders, he put to death great numbers of Romans and all the citizens of Alexandria) that he became universally hated. Even those closest to him started to fear him; and as a result he was killed by a centurion, when he was surrounded by his troops. Here it should be noted that princes cannot escape death if the attempt is made by a fanatic,[2] because anyone who has no fear of death himself can succeed in inflicting it; on the other hand, there is less need for a prince to be afraid, since such assassinations are very rare. However, the prince should restrain himself from inflicting grave injury on anyone in his service whom he has close to him in his affairs of state. That was how Antoninus erred. He put to death, with disgrace, a brother of that centurion, whom in turn he threatened every day even though still retaining him in his bodyguard. This rash behaviour was calculated to bring him grief, as in the end it did.

But let us come to Commodus, for whom ruling the empire was an easy task, since being the son of Marcus Aurelius he held it by hereditary right. He had only to follow in the footsteps of his father, and then he would have satisfied the soldiers and the people. But, as he was of a cruel, bestial disposition, he endeavoured to indulge the soldiers and make them dissolute, in order to exercise his rapacity on the people. On the other hand, he forgot his dignity, often descended into the amphitheatres to fight with the gladiators, and did other ignoble things hardly worthy of the imperial majesty; as a result the soldiers came to despise him. So, being hated on the one side and scorned on the other, he fell victim to a conspiracy which ended in his death.

It now remains for us to describe the character of Maximinus. He was a very warlike man, and the troops, being sick of the effeminacies of Alexander, whom I discussed above, elected him emperor after Alexander's death. He did not hold the empire for long, because two things made him hated and despised: first, he was of the lowest origins, having once been a shepherd in Thrace (this was well known to everybody and lowered him in everyone's eyes); second, at his accession he put off going to Rome to be formally hailed as emperor, and he impressed people as being extremely savage because he inflicted many cruelties through his prefects in Rome and in other parts of the empire. As a result, there was a universal upsurge of indignation against him because of his mean birth, and an upsurge of hatred caused by fear of his ferocity. First Africa rebelled, and then the Senate with the support of all the people of Rome. All Italy conspired against him. The conspiracy was joined by his own troops who, when they were besieging Aquileia and finding difficulties in taking the town, sickened of his cruelty; seeing how many enemies he had they feared him less, and they killed him.

I do not want to discuss Heliogabalus, or Macrinus, or Julian, who were thoroughly despised and therefore did not last long. Instead I shall conclude by saying that contemporary princes are less troubled by this problem of having to take extraordinary measures to satisfy the soldiers. They do have to give them some consideration; but notwithstanding this the problem is soon settled, because princes today do not possess standing armies which, like the armies of the Roman Empire, have become firmly established in the government and administration of conquered territories. So if in Roman times it was necessary to satisfy the demands of the soldiers rather than those of the people, this was because the soldiers had more power than the people. In our own times it is necessary for all rulers, except the Turk and the Sultan,[3] to conciliate the people rather than the soldiers, because the people are the more powerful. I make an exception of the Turk, because that ruler maintains a standing army of twelve thousand infantry and fifteen thousand cavalry, essential to the security and strength of his kingdom; and so he must subordinate every other consideration to that of retaining their loyalty. Similarly, the Sultan's dominion is completely in the hands of his soldiers, and he also, without regard for the people, must make sure of their allegiance to him. You should note that the Sultan's state differs from all the other principalities, being similar to the papacy, which cannot be called either a hereditary or a new principality. It is not the sons of the former ruler who inherit and become rulers but the one elected by those with the authority to do so. As this system is an ancient one it cannot be classified among the new principalities. There are none of the difficulties encountered in a new principality; although the prince is new, the institutions of the state are old, and they are devised to accommodate him as if he were the hereditary ruler.

But let us go back to the subject. I say that whoever follows my argument will realize that the downfall of the emperors I mentioned was caused by either hatred or scorn. He will also recognize why it happened that, some of them behaving one way and some of them another, in both cases one ended happily and the rest came to grief. As they were new princes, it was useless and disastrous for Pertinax and Alexander to want to imitate Marcus Aurelius, who succeeded by hereditary right; similarly it was fatal for Caracalla, Commodus, and Maximinus to imitate Severus, since they lacked the prowess to follow in his footsteps. Therefore, a new prince in a new principality cannot imitate the actions of Marcus Aurelius, nor is he bound to follow those of Severus. Rather, he should select from Severus the qualities necessary to establish his state, and from Marcus Aurelius those which are conducive to its maintenance and glory after it has been stabilized and made secure.

xx. *Whether fortresses and many of the other present-day expedients to which princes have recourse are useful or not*

To keep a secure hold on their states some princes have disarmed their subjects; some have kept the towns subject to them divided; some have purposely fostered animosity against themselves; some have endeavoured to win over those who were initially suspect; some have put up fortresses; some have razed them to the ground. It is impossible to give a final verdict on any of these policies, unless one examines the particular circumstances of the states in which such decisions have had to be taken. None the less, I shall as far as possible discuss the matter in generalizations.

Now, no new prince has ever at any time disarmed his subjects; rather, when he has found them unarmed he has always given them arms. This is because by arming your subjects you arm yourself; those who were suspect become loyal, and those who were loyal not only remain so but are changed from being merely your subjects to being your partisans. Then, as it is impossible to arm everybody, when you have given this privilege to some you can deal more severely with the others. And this discrimination will, when it is understood, put the former under more of an obligation; the others will excuse you, judging that it is necessary for those who run more risks and incur greater obligations to be treated more favourably. But as soon as you disarm your subjects you start to offend them, showing whether through cowardice or suspicion that you mistrust them; and on either score hatred is aroused against you.

Then, since you cannot stay unarmed, you are forced to have recourse to mercenary troops, whose character is as I described above. And even if these mercenaries were reliable, they could not be sufficiently so to protect you against powerful enemies and against subjects you distrust. So, as I said, a new prince in a new principality always arms his subjects; and history is full of examples of this.

But when a prince acquires a state which is annexed to his original principality, like a new limb, then he must disarm his new subjects, except for those who were his partisans. Even they, as time and opportunity allow, must be made weak and effeminate, and matters must be so arranged that throughout your dominions only your own soldiers, serving near you in your original dominion, are armed.

Our ancestors, and those who were considered to be wise, were accustomed to say that it was necessary to control Pistoia by means of factions and Pisa by means of fortresses; so they fostered strife in various of their subject towns, so as to control them more easily. In those days when there was stability of a sort in Italy, this was doubtless sensible; but I do not think it makes a good rule today. I do not believe that any good at all ever comes of dissension. On the contrary, on the approach of the enemy, cities which are so divided inevitably succumb at once; the weaker faction will always go over to the invader, and the other will not be able to hold out.

The Venetians, influenced I believe by the considerations I gave above, fostered the Guelf and Ghibelline factions in their subject cities.[1] Although they never allowed bloodshed, yet they fostered these discords so that the citizens, taken up with their own dissensions, might never combine against them. But, as we have seen, this did not turn out as they had planned, because when the Venetians were routed at Vailà one faction immediately summoned up courage and took the whole state from them. Such methods, therefore, argue for weakness on the part of the prince. In a strong principality such dissensions are never allowed. They profit the prince only in times of peace, when he can make use of them to handle his subjects more easily; but when war comes the weakness of this policy is revealed.

There is no doubt that a prince's greatness depends on his triumphing over difficulties and opposition. So fortune, especially when she wants to build up the greatness of a new prince, whose need to acquire standing is more pressing than that of a hereditary ruler, finds enemies for him and encourages them to take the field against him, so that he may have cause to triumph over them and ascend higher on the ladder his foes have provided. Many, therefore, believe that when he has the chance an able prince should cunningly foster some opposition to himself so that by overcoming it he can enhance his own stature.

Princes, especially new ones, have found men who were suspect at the start of their rule more loyal and more useful than those who, at the start, were their trusted friends. Pandolfo Petrucci, ruler of Siena, governed his state more with the support of those who had been suspect than with that of the others. But here generalization is impossible, because circumstances vary. I shall say just this: a prince will never have any difficulty in winning over those who were initially his enemies, when they are such that they need someone to lean upon. And they are all the more forced to serve him loyally inasmuch as they realize that it is more necessary for them to wipe out with their actions the bad opinion he had formed of them; and so the prince finds them more useful than those who feel themselves so secure in his service that they neglect his interests.

Since it is relevant to the subject, I shall remind princes who have recently seized a state for themselves through support given from within that they should carefully reflect on the motives of those who helped them. If these were not based on a natural affection for the new prince, but rather on discontent with the existing government, he will retain their friendship only with considerable difficulty and exertion, because it will be impossible for him in his turn to satisfy them. If we carefully examine the reasons for this, with examples taken from ancient and modern times, it will be found that a prince far more easily wins the friendship of those who were formerly satisfied with the existing government, and so were hostile to him then, than of those who, because they were dissatisfied, became his friends and favoured his occupation.

Princes, in order to hold their dominions more securely, have been accustomed to build fortresses, which act as a curb on those who may plot rebellion against them, and which provide a safe refuge from sudden attack. I approve of this policy, because it has been used from the time of the ancient world. None the less, in our own time, messer Niccolò Vitelli saw fit to raze two fortresses in Città di Castello, in order to maintain his hold there. Guidobaldo, duke of Urbino, after he returned to the dominion from which Cesare Borgia had chased him, razed to the ground all the fortresses in his province, in the belief that by doing so it would be more difficult for him to lose the state again, when they returned to Bologna, the Bentivoglio followed a similar policy.[2] So we see that fortresses are useful or not depending on circumstances; and if they are beneficial in one direction, they are harmful in another. It can be put like this: the prince who is more afraid of his own people than of foreign interference should build fortresses; but the prince who fears foreign interference more than his own people should forget about them. The castle of Milan, built by Francesco Sforza, has caused and will cause more uprisings against the House of Sforza than any other source of disturbance. So the best fortress that exists is to avoid being hated by the people. If you have fortresses and yet the people hate you they will not save you; once the people have taken up arms they will never lack outside help. In our own time, there is no instance of a fortress proving its worth to any ruler, except in the case of the countess of Forlì, after her consort, count Girolamo, had been killed. In her case the fortress gave her a refuge against the assault of the populace, where she could wait for succour from Milan and then recover the state. Circumstances were such that the people could not obtain support from outside. But subsequently fortresses proved of little worth even to her, when Cesare Borgia attacked her and then her hostile subjects joined forces with the invader. So then as before it would have been safer for her to have avoided the enmity of the people than to have had fortresses. So, all things considered, I commend those who erect fortresses and those who do not; and I censure anyone who, putting his trust in fortresses, does not mind if he is hated by the people.

XXI. *How a prince must act to win honour*

Nothing brings a prince more prestige than great campaigns and striking demonstrations of his personal abilities. In our own time we have Ferdinand of Aragon, the present king of Spain. He can be regarded as a new prince, because from being a weak king he has risen to being, for fame and glory, the first king of Christendom. If you study his achievements, you will find that they were all magnificent and some of them unparalleled. At the start of his reign he attacked Granada; and this campaign laid the foundation of his power.[1] First, he embarked on it undistracted, and without fear of interference; he used it to engage the energies of the barons of Castile who, as they were giving their minds to the war, had no mind for causing trouble at home. In this way, without their realizing what was happening, he increased his standing and his control over them. He was able to sustain his armies with money from the Church and the people, and, by means of that long war, to lay a good foundation for his standing army, which has subsequently won him renown. In addition, in order to be able to undertake even greater campaigns, still making use of religion, he turned his hand to a pious work of cruelty when he chased out the Moriscos and rid his kingdom of them; there could not have been a more pitiful or striking enterprise.[2] Under the same cloak of religion he assaulted Africa; he started his campaign in Italy; he has recently attacked France. Thus he has always planned and completed great projects, which have always kept his subjects in a state of suspense and wonder, and intent on their outcome. And his moves have followed closely upon one another in such a way that he has never allowed time and opportunity in between times for people to foster conspiracies against him.

It is also very profitable for a prince to give striking demonstrations of his capabilities in regard to government at home, similar to those which are attributed to messer Bernabò of Milan; in the event that someone accomplishes something exceptional, for good or evil, in civil life, he should be rewarded or punished in a way that sets everyone talking. Above all, in all his doings a prince must endeavour to win the reputation of being a great man of outstanding ability.

A prince also wins prestige for being a true friend or a true enemy, that is, for revealing himself without any reservation in favour of one side against another. This policy is always more advantageous than neutrality. For instance, if the powers neighbouring on you come to blows, either they are such that, if one of them conquers, you will be in danger, or they are not. In either case it will always be to your advantage to declare yourself and to wage a vigorous war; because, in the first case, if you do not declare yourself you will always be at the mercy of the conqueror, much to the pleasure and satisfaction of the one who has been beaten, and you will have no justification nor any way to obtain protection or refuge. The conqueror does not want doubtful friends who do not help him when he is in difficulties; the loser repudiates you because you were unwilling to go, arms in hand, and throw in your lot with him.

Antiochus went into Greece, at the invitation of the Aetolians, to drive out the Romans. He sent envoys to the Achaeans, who were friends of the Romans, to encourage them to stand aside; for their part, the Romans started persuading the Achaeans to fight with them. The matter came to be debated in the council of the Achaeans, where the ambassador of Antiochus was urging them to remain neutral. To this, the Roman legate replied: '*Quod autem isti dicunt non interponendi vos bello, nihil magis alienum rebus vestris est; sine gratia, sine dignitate, praemium victoris eritis.*'[3]

It is always the case that the one who is not your friend will request your neutrality, and that the one who is your friend will request your armed support. Princes who are irresolute usually follow the path of neutrality in order to escape immediate danger, and usually they come to grief. But when you boldly declare your support for one side, then if that side conquers, even though the victor is powerful and you are at his mercy, he is under an obligation to you and he has committed himself to friendly ties with you; and men are never so unprincipled as to deal harshly and ungratefully with you in this instance. Then again, victories are never so overwhelming that the conqueror does not have to show some scruples, especially regarding justice. If on the other hand your ally is defeated, he will shelter you; he will help you while he can, and you become associates whose joint fortunes may well change for the better. Now, in the second case, when the combatants are such that you need have no fear of the victor, there is all the more reason to support one side or the other. In this way you help destroy one combatant with the help of the other, who would be helping him himself if he were wise. If you are the victors, your ally is at your mercy, and with your help it is impossible for him not to win.

Here it is to be noted that a prince should never join in an aggressive alliance with someone more powerful than himself, unless it is a matter of necessity, as I said above. This is because if you are the victors, you emerge as his prisoner; and princes should do their utmost to escape being at the mercy of others. The Venetians joined with France against the duke of Milan, and they could have escaped making this alliance, which proved their undoing. But when such an alliance cannot be avoided (as was the case with the Florentines when the pope and Spain led their armies against Lombardy) then the prince should support one side or another for the reasons given above. Then, no government should ever imagine that it can always adopt a safe course; rather, it should regard all possible courses of action as risky. This is the way things are: whenever one tries to escape one danger one runs into another. Prudence consists in being able to assess the nature of a particular threat and in accepting the lesser evil.

A prince should also show his esteem for talent,[4] actively encouraging able men, and honouring those who excel in their profession. Then he must encourage his citizens so that they can go peaceably about their business, whether it be trade or agriculture or any other human occupation. One man should not be afraid of improving his possessions, lest they be taken away from him, or another deterred by high taxes from starting a new business. Rather, the prince should be ready to reward men who want to do these things and anyone who endeavours in any way to increase the prosperity of his city or his state. As well as this, at suitable times of the year he should entertain the people with shows and festivities. And since every city is divided into guilds or family groups, he should pay attention to these, meet them from time to time, and give an example of courtesy and munificence, while all the time, none the less, fully maintaining the dignity of his position, because this should never be wanting in anything.

XXII. *A prince's personal staff*

The choosing of ministers is a matter of no little importance for a prince; and their worth depends on the sagacity of the prince himself. The first opinion that is formed of a ruler's intelligence is based on the quality of the men he has around him. When they are competent and loyal he can always be considered wise, because he has been able to recognize their competence and to keep them loyal. But when they are otherwise, the prince is always open to adverse criticism; because his first mistake has been in the choice of his ministers.

No one who knew messer Antonio da Venafro[1] as the minister of Pandolfo Petrucci, prince of Siena, could but conclude that therefore Pandolfo was himself a man of great ability. There are three kinds of intelligence: one kind understands things for itself, the second appreciates what others can understand, the third understands neither for itself nor through others. This first kind is excellent, the second good, and the third kind useless. So it follows that Pandolfo, if he did not have the first kind of intelligence, at least had the second. If a prince has the discernment to recognize the good or bad in what another says or does, even though he has no acumen himself, he can see when his minister's actions are good or bad, and he can praise or correct accordingly; in this way, the minister cannot hope to deceive him and so takes care not to go wrong.

But as for how a prince can assess his minister, here is an infallible guide: when you see a minister thinking more of himself than of you, and seeking his own profit in everything he does, such a one will never be a good minister, you will never be able to trust him. This is because a man entrusted with the task of government must never think of himself but of the prince, and must never concern himself with anything except the prince's affairs. To keep his minister up to the mark the prince, on his side, must be considerate towards him, must pay him honour, enrich him, put him in his debt, share with him both honours and responsibilities. Thus the minister will see how dependent he is on the prince; and then having riches and honours to the point of surfeit he will desire no more; holding so many offices, he cannot but fear changes. When, therefore, relations between princes and their ministers are of this kind, they can have confidence in each other; when they are otherwise, the result is always disastrous for one or the other of them.

XXIII. *How flatterers must be shunned*

There is one important subject I do not want to pass over, the mistake which princes can only with difficulty avoid making if they are not extremely prudent or do not choose their ministers well. I am referring to flatterers, who swarm in the courts. Men are so happily absorbed in their own affairs and indulge in such self-deception that it is difficult for them not to fall victim to this plague; and some efforts to protect oneself from flatterers involve the risk of becoming despised. This is because the only way to safeguard yourself against flatterers is by letting people understand that you are not offended by the truth; but if everyone can speak the truth to you then you lose respect. So a shrewd prince should adopt a middle way, choosing wise men for his government and allowing only those the freedom to speak the truth to him, and then only concerning matters on which he asks their opinion, and nothing else. But he should also question them thoroughly and listen to what they say; then he should make up his own mind, by himself. And his attitude towards his councils and towards each one of his advisers should be such that they will recognize that the more freely they speak out the more acceptable they will be. Apart from these, the prince should heed no one; he should put the policy agreed upon into effect straight away, and he should adhere to it rigidly. Anyone who does not do this is ruined by flatterers or is constantly changing his mind because of conflicting advice: as a result he is held in low esteem.

I want to give a modern illustration of this argument. Bishop Luca, in the service of Maximilian the present emperor, said of his majesty that he never consulted anybody and never did things as he wanted to; this happened because he did the opposite of what I said above. The emperor is a secretive man, he does not tell anyone of his plans, and he accepts no advice. But as soon as he puts his plans into effect, and they come to be known, they meet with opposition from those around him; and then he is only too easily diverted from his purpose. The result is that whatever he does one day is undone the next, what he wants or plans to do is never clear, and no reliance can be placed on his decisions.

A prince must, therefore, never lack advice. But he must take it when he wants to, not when others want him to; indeed, he must discourage everyone from tendering advice about anything unless it is asked for. All the same, he should be a constant questioner, and he must listen patiently to the truth regarding what he has inquired about. Moreover, if he finds that anyone for some reason holds the truth back he must show his wrath. And though many suppose that a prince may rightly be esteemed shrewd not because he is so himself but because of the quality of those there to advise him, they are undoubtedly mistaken. For this is an infallible rule: a prince who is not himself wise cannot be well advised, unless he happens to put himself in the hands of one individual who looks after all his affairs and is an extremely shrewd man. In this case, he may well be given good advice, but he would not last long because the man who governs for him would soon deprive him of his state. But when seeking advice of more than one person a prince who is not himself wise will never get unanimity in his councils or be able to reconcile their views. Each councillor will consult his own interests; and the prince will not know how to correct or understand them. Things cannot be otherwise, since men will always do badly by you unless they are forced to be virtuous. So the conclusion is that good advice, whomever it comes from, depends on the shrewdness of the prince who seeks it, and not the shrewdness of the prince on good advice.

XXIV. *Why the Italian princes have lost their states*

If he carefully observes the rules I have given above, a new prince will appear to have been long established and will quickly become more safe and secure in his government than if he had been ruling his state for a long time. The actions of a new prince attract much more attention than those of a hereditary ruler; and when these actions are marked by prowess they, far more than royal blood, win men over and capture their allegiance. This is because men are won over by the present far more than by the past; and when they decide that what is being done here and now is good, they content themselves with that and do not go looking for anything else. Indeed in that case they would do anything to defend their prince, provided he himself is not deficient in other things. Thus the new prince will have a twofold glory, in having founded a new state and in having adorned and strengthened it with good laws, sound defences, reliable allies, and inspiring leadership, just as the one who is born a prince and loses his state through incompetence is shamed twice over.

Let us consider those Italian rulers, such as the king of Naples, the duke of Milan, and so forth who have lost their states in our own times. If we do so, we shall find that they shared, first, a common weakness in regard to their military organizations, for the reasons fully discussed above. Then, it will be found that some of them incurred the hostility of the people or, if they had the people on their side, they did not know how to keep the allegiance of the nobles. If they are not undermined in one of these ways, states which are robust enough to keep an army in the field cannot be lost. Philip of Macedon (not the father of Alexander but the one who was conquered by Titus Quintius) ruled a minor dominion in comparison with the greatness of the Romans who attacked him with Greek auxiliaries. None the less, as he was a military man, who knew how to content the people and keep the allegiance of the nobles, he sustained the war against them for many years; and although at the end he lost control of some cities, he still kept his kingdom.

So these princes of ours, whose power had been established many years, may not blame fortune for their losses. Their own indolence was to blame, because, having never imagined when times were quiet that they could change (and this is a common failing of mankind, never to anticipate a storm when the sea is calm), when adversity came their first thoughts were of flight and not of resistance. They hoped that the people, revolted by the outrages of the conqueror, would recall them. Now this policy, when all else fails, is all to the good. But it is wrong to have neglected other precautions in that hope: we do not find men falling down just because they expect to find someone helping them up. It may not happen; and, if it does happen, it leaves you unsafe because your expedient was cowardly and not based on your own actions. The only sound, sure, and enduring methods of defence are those based on your own actions and prowess.

XXV. *How far human affairs are governed by fortune, and how fortune can be opposed*

I am not unaware that many have held and hold the opinion that events are controlled by fortune and by God in such a way that the prudence of men cannot modify them, indeed, that men have no influence whatsoever. Because of this, they would conclude that there is no point in sweating over things, but that one should submit to the rulings of chance. This opinion has been more widely held in our own times, because of the great changes and variations, beyond human imagining, which we have experienced and experience every day. Sometimes, when thinking of this, I have myself inclined to this same opinion. None the less, so as not to rule out our free will, I believe that it is probably true that fortune is the arbiter of half the things we do, leaving the other half or so to be controlled by ourselves. I compare fortune to one of those violent rivers which, when they are enraged, flood the plains, tear down trees and buildings, wash soil from one place to deposit it in another. Everyone flees before them, everybody yields to their impetus, there is no possibility of resistance. Yet although such is their nature, it does not follow that when they are flowing quietly one cannot take precautions, constructing dykes and embankments so that when the river is in flood they would keep to one channel or their impetus be less wild and dangerous. So it is with fortune. She shows her potency where there is no well-regulated power to resist her, and her impetus is felt where she knows there are no embankments and dykes built to restrain her. If you consider Italy, the theatre of those changes and variations I mentioned, which first appeared here, you will see that she is a country without embankments and without dykes: for if Italy had been adequately reinforced, like Germany, Spain, and France, either this flood would not have caused the great changes it has, or it would not have swept in at all.

I want what I have said to suffice, in general terms, on the question of how to oppose fortune. But, confining myself now to particular circumstances, I say that we see that some princes flourish one day and come to grief the next, without appearing to have changed in character or any other way. This I believe arises, first, for the reasons discussed at length earlier on, namely, that those princes who are utterly dependent on fortune come to grief when their fortune changes. I also believe that the one who adapts his policy to the times prospers, and likewise that the one whose policy clashes with the demands of the times does not. It can be observed that men use various methods in pursuing their own personal objectives, that is glory and riches. One man proceeds with circumspection, another impetuously; one uses violence, another stratagem; one man goes about things patiently, another does the opposite; and yet everyone, for all this diversity of method, can reach his objective. It can also be observed that with two circumspect men, one will achieve his end, the other not; and likewise two men succeed equally well with different methods, one of them being circumspect and the other impetuous. This results from nothing else except the extent to which their methods are or are not suited to the nature of the times. Thus it happens that, as I have said, two men, working in different ways, can achieve the same end, and of two men working in the same way one gets what he wants and the other does not. This also explains why prosperity is ephemeral; because if a man behaves with patience and circumspection and the time and circumstances are such that this method is called for, he will prosper; but if time and circumstances change he will be ruined because he does not change his policy. Nor do we find any man shrewd enough to know how to adapt his policy in this way; either because he cannot do otherwise than what is in character or because, having always prospered by proceeding one way, he cannot persuade himself to change. Thus a man who is circumspect, when circumstances demand impetuous behaviour, is unequal to the task, and so he comes to grief. If he changed his character according to the time and circumstances, then his fortune would not change.

Pope Julius II was impetuous in everything; and he found the time and circumstances so favourable to his way of proceeding that he always met with success. Consider his first campaign, against Bologna, when messer Giovanni Bentivogli was still living. The Venetians mistrusted it: so did the king of Spain; and Julius was still arguing about the enterprise with France. None the less, with typical forcefulness and impetuosity, he launched the expedition in person. This move disconcerted and arrested Spain and the Venetians, the latter because they were afraid and the former because of the king's ambition to reconquer all the kingdom of Naples. On the other hand, he drew the king of France after him. This was because the king, seeing Julius go into action, and anxious for his support in subduing the Venetians, decided he could not refuse him troops without doing him a manifest disservice. With that impetuous move of his, therefore, Julius achieved what no other pontiff, with the utmost human prudence, would have achieved. Because had Julius delayed setting out from Rome until all his plans and negotiations were completed, as any other pontiff would have done, he would never have succeeded. The king of France would have found a hundred and one excuses, and the others would have inspired Julius with a hundred and one fears. I shall not discuss his other deeds, which were all like this and which all met with success. The brevity of his pontifical life did not let him experience the contrary. If there had come a time when it was necessary for him to act with circumspection he would have come to grief: he would never have acted other than in character.

I conclude, therefore, that as fortune is changeable whereas men are obstinate in their ways, men prosper so long as fortune and policy are in accord, and when there is a clash they fail. I hold strongly to this: that it is better to be impetuous than circumspect; because fortune is a woman and if she is to be submissive it is necessary to beat and coerce her. Experience shows that she is more often subdued by men who do this than by those who act coldly. Always, being a woman, she favours young men, because they are less circumspect and more ardent, and because they command her with greater audacity.

XXVI. *Exhortation to liberate Italy from the barbarians*

After deliberating on all the things discussed above, I asked myself whether in present-day Italy the times were propitious to honour a new prince, and whether the circumstances existed here which would make it possible for a prudent and capable man to introduce a new order, bringing honour to himself and prosperity to all the Italians. Well, I believe that so many things conspire to favour a new prince, that I cannot imagine there ever was a time more suitable than the present. And if, as I said, the Israelites had to be enslaved in Egypt for Moses to emerge as their forceful leader; if the Persians had to be oppressed by the Medes so that the greatness of Cyrus could be recognized; if the Athenians had to be scattered to demonstrate the excellence of Theseus: then, at the present time, in order to discover the worth of an Italian spirit, Italy had to be brought to her present extremity. She had to be more enslaved than the Hebrews, more oppressed than the Persians, more widely scattered than the Athenians; leaderless, lawless, crushed, despoiled, torn, overrun; she had to have endured every kind of desolation.

And although before now there was a man in whom some spark seemed to show that he was ordained by God to redeem the country,[1] none the less it was seen how afterwards, at the very height of his career, he was rejected by fortune. So now, left lifeless, Italy is waiting to see who can be the one to heal her wounds, put an end to the sacking of Lombardy, to extortion in the Kingdom and in Tuscany, and cleanse those sores which have now been festering for so long. See how Italy beseeches God to send someone to save her from those barbarous cruelties and outrages; see how eager and willing the country is to follow a banner, if only someone will raise it. And at the present time it is impossible to see in what she can place more hope than in your illustrious House, which, with its fortune and prowess, favoured by God and by the Church, of which it is now the head, can lead Italy to her salvation. The task will not be very hard, if you will call to mind the actions and lives of the men I have mentioned.[2] These men may be exceptional and remarkable; they were men none the less, and each of them had less opportunity than is offered now. Their enterprise was neither more just nor easier, and God was no more their friend than he is yours. There is great justice in our cause: *iustum enim est bellum quibus necessarium, et pia arma ubi nulla nisi in armis spes est.*[3] There is the greatest readiness, and where that is so there cannot be great difficulty, provided only your House will emulate the methods of those I have singled out for admiration. As well as this, unheard of wonders are to be seen, performed by God: the sea is divided, a cloud has shown you the way, water has gushed from the rock, it has rained manna; all things have conspired to your greatness. The rest is up to you. God does not want to do everything Himself, and take away from us our free will and our share of the glory which belongs to us.

It is not to be marvelled at that none of the Italians I have named has succeeded in doing what, it is hoped, your illustrious House will do, or that in so many revolutions in Italy and so many martial campaigns it has always seemed that our military prowess has been extinguished. This is because the old military systems were bad and there has been no one who knew how to establish a new one. And nothing brings a man greater honour than the new laws and new institutions he establishes. When these are soundly based and bear the mark of greatness, they make him revered and admired. Now, in Italy the opportunities are not wanting for thorough reorganization. Here we would find greater prowess among those who follow, were it not lacking among the leaders. Look at the duels and the combats between a few, how the Italians are superior in strength, in skill, in inventiveness; but when it is a matter of armies, they do not compare. All this is because of the weakness of the leaders. Those who are capable are not obeyed. Everyone imagines he is competent, and hitherto no one has had the competence to dominate the others by his prowess and good fortune. As a result of this, over so long a time, in so many wars during the past twenty years, when there has been an all-Italian army it has always given a bad account of itself, as witness the battles of Taro, then Alessandria, Capua, Genoa, Vailà, Bologna, and Mestre.[4]

Therefore if your illustrious House wants to emulate those eminent men who saved their countries, before all else it is essential for it, as the right basis for every campaign, to raise a citizen army; for there can be no more loyal, more true, or better troops. Taken singly, these troops are good; acting as a united army, when they find themselves under the command of their own prince and honoured and maintained by him, they are still better. It is necessary, therefore, to raise such an army, in order to base our defence against the invaders on Italian strength. Although the Swiss and Spanish infantry may be considered formidable, none the less there are faults in both which would enable a third kind of army not only to hold them in battle but to be sure of conquering. The Spaniards cannot withstand cavalry, and the Swiss have cause to fear infantrymen who meet them in combat with a determination equal to their own. Thus it has been found, and experience will prove, that the Spaniards cannot withstand French cavalry and the Swiss succumb to Spanish infantry. There may have been no complete demonstration of this latter assertion, but there was some indication of its truth at the battle of Ravenna, where Spanish infantry troops clashed with the German battalions, which adopt the same line of battle as the Swiss. In the encounter, the Spaniards, making good use of their bucklers, with great agility thrust their way between and under the German pikes, and attacked with impunity while the Germans were defenceless. If it had not been for the cavalry which charged them, the Spaniards would have annihilated the Germans.[5] So, having grasped the defects of these Swiss and Spanish infantry, you can develop a new type, capable of withstanding cavalry and undaunted by other infantry. This will be ensured by raising new armies and employing new formations. It is things of this kind which, when newly introduced, bring a new prince greatness and prestige.

In order therefore that Italy, after so long a time, may behold its saviour, this opportunity must not be let slip. And I cannot express with what love he would be welcomed in all those provinces which have suffered from these foreign inundations, with what thirst for vengeance, with what resolute loyalty, with what devotion and tears. What doors would be closed to him? What people would deny him their obedience? What envy should stand in his way? What Italian would refuse him allegiance? This barbarous tyranny stinks in everyone's nostrils. Let your illustrious House undertake this task, therefore, with the courage and hope which belong to just enterprises, so that, under your standard, our country may be ennobled, and under your auspices what Petrarch said may come to pass:

> *Vertue 'gainst fury shall advance the fight,*
> *And it i' th' combate soone shall put to flight:*
> *For th' old Romane valour is not dead,*
> *Nor in th' Italians brests extinguished.*[6]

GLOSSARY OF PROPER NAMES

The reader who wants a fairly compact account of the general historical background to the period will find Volume I of the NEW CAMBRIDGE MODERN HISTORY *(The Renaissance 1493–1520) very helpful.*

ACHILLES. Hero of the *Iliad*, educated by Phoenix and Chiron the centaur.

ACUTO, GIOVANNI. Italianization of the name of John Hawkwood, an Essex man who served in France and was knighted by Edward III. In 1360 he went with a small force of his own to Italy, where he established an enduring reputation as a *condottiere*. It has been suggested that the Italian proverb *Inglese italianato è un diavolo incarnato* (the Italianized Englishman is a devil incarnate) first referred to the outrages perpetrated by English mercenaries of his kind.

AGATHOCLES. Declared ruler of Syracuse in 317 BC, and extended his authority over all Sicily except for territory dominated by Carthage. In 310 BC defeated by a Carthaginian army under Hamilcar which then besieged Syracuse itself. He successfully carried the war into Africa, but was forced to return home when several cities in Syracuse revolted against him, and was constrained to make peace with Carthage. Died in 289 BC. Machiavelli's account is taken from the Roman historian, Justin.

ALEXANDER. Alexander the Great, king of Macedonia (356–323 BC). Ascended the throne 336. Subdued Greece and crossed the Hellespont against Persia 334. Defeated Darius *c.* 333. Made himself master of Asia and invaded India 327.

ALEXANDER. M. Aurelius Alexander Severus, Roman emperor AD 222–35. First cousin of the emperor Heliogabalus, by whom he was adopted in 221. He was murdered by mutinous troops, possibly at the instigation of Maximinus.

ALEXANDER VI. Cardinal Rodrigo Borgia elected pope in 1492 and died in 1503. Notorious for the corruptness of his personal life and his fanatical devotion to his illegitimate children. But he was an able administrator, the first pope to be challenged by a French invasion of Italy and a Franco-Spanish war.

ANTIOCHUS. Antiochus the Great, king of Syria, 223–187 BC. Continually involved in hostilities with the Romans.

ASCANIO. See Sforza, Cardinal.

BAGLIONI, THE. Rulers of the papal city of Perugia, where their power was established in the fifteenth century.

BENTIVOGLI, GIOVANNI (1438–1508). Son of Annibale Bentivogli, the leading citizen of Bologna who was murdered by a rival faction in 1445. In 1462 he made himself ruler of Bologna. In 1499 he sent his son, Annibale, to submit to Louis XII, after the fall of Milan. He was driven from the city in 1506 by Julius II when the latter was asserting his claims on the cities of the Romagna. Died in exile. His sons were restored to Bologna by the French in 1511, but Bologna again fell to Julius in 1512. The events to which Machiavelli refers in chapter XIX took place in 1445.

BERGAMO, BARTOLOMMEO DA. Bartolommeo Colleone da Bergamo, Mercenary in the service of Venice from 1424. Commanded the Venetian forces after the disgrace of Carmagnola. Died 1475.

BERNABÒ, MESSER. Bernabò Visconti, who ruled the Milanese territories (1354–85) in conjunction with his two brothers. Imprisoned in 1385, and subsequently killed, by his nephew Gian Galeazzo.

BORGIA, CESARE. Born in Rome *c.* 1476, son of Cardinal Rodrigo Borgia and his mistress Vannozza Catanei. He was never a priest, but was created a cardinal after he had become a deacon in 1493. In 1498 renounced his vows, before travelling to France to negotiate a treaty between Alexander VI and Louis XII, giving Louis a dispensation to marry the widow of Charles VIII and an alliance with the papacy for the conquest of Naples. Was created duke of Valence, and married Charlotte d'Albret, the king's cousin. Louis promised him support in his projected conquest of the Romagna which, nominally under the suzerainty of the pope, was controlled by independent tyrants. By the spring of 1501 Cesare had subdued the seven towns of Fano, Pesaro, Rimini, Cesena, Forlì, Faenza, and Imola, and the pope created him duke of Romagna. In 1502, the pope planned the conquest of Camerino and Urbino. After a successful campaign, Cesare faced a revolt by his own mercenaries, which he crushed brilliantly and ruthlessly at Sinigaglia, in the late winter of 1502. In 1503 the pope died; Cesare's state crumbled with the death of his father – although the Romagna was apparently notably loyal – and after various bravely endured misfortunes he eventually died in Spain in 1507.

Machiavelli was able to study Cesare at first hand: he was sent on missions to him in 1502, and studied closely the methods Cesare used to trick his rebellious mercenaries, and he saw him again after his fall, in Rome. The 'idealization' of Cesare Borgia in *The Prince*, does not imply that Machiavelli in any way distorted the facts about Cesare Borgia as he knew them. He did magnify his stature.

BRACCIO. Andrea Braccio da Montone (1368–1424). *Condottiere* trained under Alberico da Barbiano. Died fighting against the forces of Joanna of Naples.

CANNESCHI. Powerful family of Bologna, supporting Milan's influence against that of Venice and Florence. In 1445 the head of the family tried to seize power against the rival Bentivogli. Annibale Bentivogli was killed, but the populace resisted and the Canneschi were driven from the city.

CARACALLA. M. Aurelius Antoninus, Roman Emperor AD 211–17. Son of the emperor Severus, he and his brother Geta succeeded on their father's death. In AD 212 murdered Geta and took sole command, which he used atrociously. To increase revenue extended Roman citizenship to all free citizens of the Empire. Murdered at the instigation of Macrinus.

CARMAGNOLA. Francesco Bussone, count of Carmagnola, where he was born *c*. 1390. Hired as a mercenary by Venice in 1425, at one time he commanded the allied forces of Venice and Florence, but became suspected of treachery and was executed at Venice in 1432.

CHARLES VII (1422–61). King of France during whose reign the English lost all their French possessions save Calais. Responsible for a number of financial and military reforms which effectively strengthened the power of the monarchy.

CHARLES VIII (1470–98). Became effective ruler of France in 1492, having married the Duchess of Brittany the year before. Invaded Italy (under the impulse of a rather vague craving for glory and dominion) in 1494 in order to assert his claim to the throne of Naples, as heir of the House of Anjou. Entered Naples in 1495. An Italian league – including

Spain and the emperor – was formed to cut off his retreat, but although the Italians were numerically superior the French got to the north safely after the drawn battle of Fornovo. In 1496, the remaining French forces were compelled to evacuate Naples. Died while preparing a second expedition against Naples.

COLONNA, CARDINAL. Giovanni, son of Antonio Colonna, prince of Salerno. Created a cardinal in 1480. Intrigued with Charles VIII against Alexander VI. Died in 1508.

COLONNA, THE. Noble Roman family, first prominent in the thirteenth century. Excommunicated and their estates confiscated by Alexander VI.

COMMODUS. M. Commodus Antoninus, Roman emperor AD 180–93. Succeeded his father, Marcus Aurelius, but was sharply contrasted in character, his reign being marked by unbridled cruelty. Strangled by a wrestler, Narcissus, at the instigation of his mistress and other members of the household.

CONIO, ALBERIGO DA. Alberigo da Barbiano, count of Cunio in the Romagna. Largely because of him the foreign mercenary troops in Italy in the last quarter of the fourteenth century were displaced by Italian *condottieri*. He formed a military company, called the Company of St George, into which he admitted only Italians. Died in 1409.

CYRUS. Founder of the Persian Empire. Killed in battle 529 BC.

DARIUS. Last king of Persia 336–331 BC.

DAVID (*c.* 1012–972 BC). Succeeded Saul as king of Israel and extended its territory by a series of brilliant military victories. Captured Jerusalem where he established the national capital.

EPAMINONDAS. Fourth-century Theban general and statesman who won for Thebes the hegemony of Greece.

FABIUS MAXIMUS. Five times consul of Rome, appointed dictator in 217 BC during defensive period of the war against Hannibal, when he was notorious for his cautious policy. An opponent of Scipio. Died 203 BC.

FERDINAND OF ARAGON (1452–1516). His marriage with Isabella of Castile proved a decisive step in the foundation of Spanish world power in the fifteenth century. After 1474 he ruled Castile as joint sovereign with Isabella, and in 1479 he succeeded as king of Aragon. In 1491, Granada, the last kingdom of the Moors in Spain, was finally conquered. Ferdinand's centralizing policy at home was accompanied by a foreign policy chiefly aimed at the encirclement of France. Entered into a compact with the French for the partition of Naples, and by 1505 had secured control of the whole territory. Succeeded by his grandson, Charles of Austria, the emperor Charles V.

FERRARA, DUKE OF. (1) Ercole d'Este, ruler of Ferrara, 1471–1505. Succeeded his half-brother Borso d'Este who was the first duke, although the family had been established at Ferrara since the early thirteenth century. Married the daughter of King Ferrante of Naples. Economic disputes with Venice and the feudal claims of the papacy led to a coalition of the Venetians and Sixtus IV against Ferrante and Ercole in 1481. The war, which involved a large number of Italian states, ended with severe territorial losses for Ferrara, after Sixtus had changed sides. In 1499, after the French conquest of Milan, he attended the French court and obtained French protection. Was succeeded by (2), Alfonso d'Este. Joined the League of Cambray (cf. Louis XII) in 1508. He remained an ally of France after the reconciliation of Julius II with Venice in 1510 and was excommunicated and attacked by Julius. Died 1534.

FILIPPO, DUKE. Filippo Visconti, last of the Visconti dukes of Milan, 1412–47. Married his daughter, Bianca, to Francesco Sforza.

FOGLIANI, GIOVANNI. Leading citizen of Fermo, killed in 1501.

FORLÌ, COUNTESS OF. Caterina Sforza (1463–1509). Natural daughter of Galeazzo Sforza and Lucrezia Landriani. Married Girolamo Riario, count of Forlì, and held power after her husband was assassinated in 1488 until Forlì was taken by Cesare Borgia in 1500. Imprisoned in Rome. Eventually died in a French convent.

GRACCHI, THE. Celebrated Roman family. Tiberius Gracchus (tribune of the plebs, 133 BC) was assassinated after he had endeavoured to limit the power of the aristocracy. His brother, C. Sempronius Gracchus (tribune of the plebs, 123 BC), tried to push through extensive reforms, was bitterly opposed to the Senate which eventually won over the people, and after a riot in which large numbers of his followers were slain, he died by the hand of his own slave.

GUIDOBALDO, DUKE OF URBINO (1472–1508). Last duke of the Montefeltro line, ruled Urbino from 1482. Fled on the approach of Cesare Borgia in 1502, returning to the city when Cesare's mercenaries formed their conspiracy against the latter. His court inspired the famous *Book of the Courtier*, a discussion of the qualities of the perfect courtier, by Baldassare Castiglione.

HAMILCAR. Hamilcar Barca, appointed commander of the Carthaginian forces in Sicily in 247 BC, during the First Punic War.

HANNIBAL (247–183 BC). Son of Hamilcar. His life was spent in continual warfare with the Romans. Became commander of the Carthaginian army in 221, invaded Italy from the north in the Second Punic War, but failed to subdue Rome, and was eventually decisively defeated in Africa. Forced to flee from Carthage and poisoned himself to escape capture by the Romans.

HELIOGABALUS, OR ELAGABALUS. Roman emperor AD 218–22. Called Heliogabalus because in his childhood he was made a priest in a cult worshipping the Sun-god Heliogabalus. His grandmother claimed that he was the son of Caracalla and a short campaign led to the defeat of Macrinus and his installation as emperor with the name M. Aurelius Antoninus, at the age of thirteen. A stupid and brutal ruler, finally murdered by his troops.

HIERO OF SYRACUSE. Hiero II of Syracuse. A member of the nobility, voluntarily elected as ruler in 270 BC after the defeat of the Mamertines (Mamertina is now Messina). Supported the Carthaginians at the start of the First Punic War, but subsequently made peace with the Romans whose ally he remained. Machiavelli's account is taken from Justin.

JOANNA, QUEEN. Joanna II of Naples. A feeble ruler during whose reign (1414–35) Naples was in continual disorder. She adopted the king of Aragon as her heir, then changed her mind and adopted Louis of Anjou, who was backed by the papacy. In the resultant conflict, the two *condottieri*, Sforza and Braccio, fought on opposite sides. She died childless, finally naming René of Provence, Louis' brother, as her successor. The kingdom was eventually won by the Aragonese.

JULIAN. M. Didus Julianus, created Roman emperor by the Praetorian Guards after the murder of Pertinax in AD 193. Was put to death on the arrival of Severus before Rome.

JULIUS II. Giuliano della Rovere, cardinal of San Pietro ad Vincula. Reigned as pope 1503–13. Succeeded Cardinal Francesco Piccolomini who reigned for a few months as Pius III after Alexander VI. He was a vigorous leader, an intelligent diplomatist and general, who fairly successfully strengthened the territorial power of the Church. He effectively crushed the power of the Roman barons, initially turned against Venice, then negotiated an anti-French alliance. At Rome he set in motion grandiose schemes for building and sculpture, destroying the ancient Basilica of St Peter and laying the foundation stone of St Peter's as it is today.

JULIUS CAESAR. Born *c.* 102 BC. As Machiavelli suggests, he initially founded his power on the favour of the people whom he won over by extravagant liberality. He made himself dictator of Rome; was assassinated in 44 BC.

LEO X (1475–1521). Cardinal Giovanni de' Medici, son of Lorenzo de' Medici. Elected pope in 1513, he vigorously promoted the fortunes of the Medici family, creating six near relations as cardinals and, for example, installing his own nephew, Lorenzo, as duke of Urbino in place of Francesco della Rovere. Initially continued the anti-French policy of Julius II, then came to terms with Francis I and completed the reconciliation with the Concordat of 1516, after which he supported the French against Charles V. A munificent patron of the arts. During his pontificate Luther published his ninety-five theses against indulgences.

LOUIS XI (1423–83). King of France from 1461. Added substantially to the territory of the French crown. The treaty which gave him the right to levy troops in Switzerland was concluded in 1474.

LOUIS XII (1462–1515). The son of Charles d'Orléans, he succeeded Charles VIII as king of France in 1498. Inherited claims upon Milan and Naples, and lost no time in asserting them. One of his first acts was to strike a bargain with Alexander VI which enabled him to renounce his wife Jeanne, daughter of Louis XI, and marry Charles's widow, who brought him Brittany as her dowry. In 1499 he concluded a treaty with Venice for the partition of Milanese territory, and he rode into Milan in the autumn of the same year. (Duke Ludovico recovered the town for a brief spell early in 1500.) In November 1500, Louis signed his secret compact with Spain for the partition of Naples, which the French invaded in 1501. The following year the two powers clashed, and in 1503 the French were routed as Garigliano. A few years later, Louis entered into a treaty with the pope, Spain, and the Empire for the partition of Venetian territories (the League of Cambray). The Venetians were completely defeated by the French army in 1509, at the battle of Agnadello (or Vailà); but having attained their objects the French grew luke-warm in the war, and Julius II started to draw closer to the Venetians. Hostility between France and the papacy intensified, and culminated in the attempt by Louis to summon a General Council (a miserable failure) and the successful formation by Julius of the Holy League. In 1512, the French won the battle of Ravenna but lost their commander, Gaston de Foix. After Ravenna, the French steadily retreated until they were left with only the Castello of Milan and the Casteletto of Genoa of all Louis' Italian conquests. (In 1512 Florence was forced to take back the Medici, and in 1513 Julius died.) In 1513, Louis concluded an alliance with Venice against Milan, but the French were defeated at the battle of Novara, by Swiss troops in the pay of Massimiliano Sforza. Early in 1515, Louis was succeeded by Francis I, who crossed the Alps at the head of a large army a few months after his accession.

LUCA, BISHOP. 'Prc' Luca', as Machiavelli calls him (*pre*' is a Venetian abbreviation of *prete*, or priest) was Luca Rainaldi, who served the emperor Maximilian as an ambassador.

LUDOVICO. Ludovico il Moro, son of Francesco Sforza, duke of Milan, and Bianca Maria Visconti. Seized power at Milan after a regency had been established for his nephew, Gian Galeazzo in 1476; married Beatrice d'Este, daughter of the duke of Ferrara, and strengthened his position by alliance with Naples and Florence. The marriage of Gian Galeazzo with Isabella of Aragon led to pressure from Naples in favour of the former, which pushed Ludovico closer to France. He favoured the invasion of Charles VIII; soon after the invasion, Gian Galeazzo died, possibly killed by Ludovico who had himself proclaimed duke. Frightened by the success of the French invasion, he joined the League of Venice in 1495. After the retreat of the French, he concluded a separate peace with them. On his accession Louis XII (who had already as duke of Orleans assumed the title of duke of Milan) asserted his claim to Milan, which he entered in 1499. A year later there was a rebellion and Ludovico returned, only to be defeated again by a new French army in 1500. He was imprisoned for the rest of his life in a French dungeon.

MACRINUS. M. Opilius Macrinus. Roman emperor AD 217–18. Rose from poor origins to the service of Severus and then became prefect under Caracalla after whose death he was proclaimed emperor. He was defeated by the supporters of Heliogabalus, and killed.

MANTUA, MARQUIS OF. Francesco Gonzaga, *condottiere* who commanded the Italian forces at the battle of Fornovo in 1495.

MARCUS AURELIUS (AD 121–80). M. Aurelius Antoninus, Roman

emperor AD 161–80. A Stoic, whose reign was marked by persecution of the Christians. The *Meditations* contains his philosophical ideals. An efficient ruler, and a hard worker, during a period when the empire was faced by grave external and internal problems.

MAXIMILIAN (1459–1519). Son and successor of the emperor Frederick III. Elected king of the Romans in 1486, was never crowned emperor at Rome, but in 1508 assumed the title of emperor-elect, with the consent of Julius II. His life was spent engaged in tortuous diplomacy designed to establish the European influence of the Habsburgs. At home, he was moderately successful in experiments aiming at unification and administrative centralization. But his ambitions were too wide, and his reign was in the end marked by frustration and failure. This was so with his dream of leading a European crusade against Islam, and with his efforts to re-establish imperial power in Italy. His incursions into Italy were mostly inspired by the desire to regain territory from the Venetians: but a continual lack of funds and the danger from French military success made a consistent policy impossible. Did not oppose the French invasion of Italy in 1494, probably hoping for the support of Charles VIII against Venice. However, in 1495 he joined the League of Venice for the expulsion of the French, although his forces were notably absent at the battle of Fornovo. In 1496 Ludovico of Milan and the Venetians offered him a subsidy to fight on their behalf in Italy against the French; by the time he came, the French invasion had failed to materialize and Ludovico engaged him on the ludicrously unsuccessful task of helping Pisa against Florentine attack. His attempt to organize a war against Louis XII, on the latter's accession, was likewise a failure and then his plans were thoroughly upset by conflict with the Swiss, the final upshot of which was the establishment of an independent, neutral Swiss Confederation. In 1507 Maximilian returned to the project of reviving the empire in Italy; he had to abandon his scheme to journey to Rome to be crowned emperor, but started hostilities with Venice which lasted on and off for about eight years. In 1512 joined the Holy League, and was active again in Italy after the accession of Francis I and the reannexation of Milan by the French in 1515, but again his efforts were unrewarded. His grandson was the emperor Charles V.

MAXIMINUS. C. Julius Verus Maximinus, Roman emperor AD 235–8. He was given high military office by, and he succeeded, Alexander

Severus, for whose murder he may have been responsible. His brief reign was cruel and bloody. Slain by his own troops.

NABIS. Tyrant of Sparta, noted for his cruelty. Succeeded 207 BC. Was defeated in battle by Philopoemen in 192 and soon after assassinated.

OLIVEROTTO OF FERMO. Oliverotto Euffreducci. Events at Fermo which Machiavelli describes took place in 1501. He was strangled at Sinigaglia in 1502.

ORCO, REMIRRO DE. Ramiro de Lorqua. Majordomo of Cesare Borgia. Accompanied him to France in 1498. Appointed governor of the Romagna in 1501. Was found dead in 1502.

ORSINI, THE. Roman family, which grew powerful during the second half of the thirteenth century. Used as mercenaries by Cesare Borgia in his early campaigns. Involved in the conspiracy against Cesare and tricked by him at Sinigaglia.

PAULO, SIGNOR. Paulo Orsini, head of the Orsini faction until he was strangled at Sinigaglia after being tricked by Cesare Borgia.

PERTINAX. P. Helvius Pertinax, Roman emperor for a few months in AD 193, having been persuaded to assume power after the death of Commodus. His impetuous reforms – especially regarding army discipline – soon alienated the Praetorian Guards and he was killed by mutinous troops.

PETRARCH. Franceso Petrarcha (1304–74). One of the greatest Italian poets, with whom Machiavelli was very familiar and whom he often quotes. The four lines at the end of *The Prince* are taken from Canzone XVI (beginning *Italia mia . . .*) which, addressed to the rulers of Italy, constitutes a protest against their internecine warfare and the employment of foreign mercenaries.

PETRUCCI, PANDOLFO. Ruler of Siena of which he made himself master in 1502. A doubtful ally of Florence. Machiavelli was sent to negotiate with him on several occasions.

PHILIP OF MACEDON. (1) King of Macedon 359–336 BC. Pursued aggressive expansionist policy, subduing the rest of Greece. Murdered while preparing to lead the Greek forces against Persia.

(2) King of Macedon 220–178 BC. Engaged in two wars against the Romans, by whom he was finally defeated in 197.

PHILOPOEMEN. Celebrated general of the Achaean League, who endeavoured to establish the independence of the Archaeans on a sound military basis. He was first elected general 208 BC.

PITIGLIANO, COUNT OF. Niccolò Orsini (1442–1510). Mercenary in the service of the Venetians, joint commander at the battle of Vailà.

PYRRHUS (318–272 BC). King of Epirus, who attempted to conquer Macedonia. Waged war against the Romans in Italy and the Carthaginians in Sicily.

ROMULUS. Legendary founder and first king of Rome.

ROUEN. Georges d'Amboise, archbishop of Rouen (1460–1510). The most influential adviser of Louis XII who particularly guided his enterprises in Italy. Made a cardinal in 1498 by Alexander VI as part of a bargain struck between him and Louis.

SAN GIORGIO. Cardinal Raffaello Riario of Savona.

SAN PIETRO AD VINCULA. See Julius II.

SAN SEVERINO, RUBERTO DA. The bastard of a Neapolitan baron, he engaged in mercenary warfare in Lombardy. Appointed commander of the Venetian forces in 1482 and later served the papacy. Died fighting in the pay of Venice in 1487.

SAUL. Chosen first king of Israel, about 1025 BC.

SAVONAROLA, GIROLAMO (1452–98). Born at Ferrara, and entered the Order of Friars Preachers (Dominicans). The early part of his life was spent quietly. In the early 1480s he was sent to the San Marco monastery at Florence, where to start with he made little impression. But from about 1491, when he became prior of San Marco, his preaching – prophetic and denunciatory – secured him a large following. After the expulsion of the Medici, when his warnings had apparently been justified, his political influence grew steadily, and was at its greatest from 1494 to 1497. The republican constitution adopted in 1494 was largely of his making. He aroused bitter opposition, as well as fanatical devotion. His persistent, open defiance of the Church provoked Alexander VI first to forbid him to preach, and eventually to excommunicate him. Opinion in Florence swiftly turned against him. In 1498 after Alexander had threatened to place Florence under an interdict, he was imprisoned, tortured, and executed.

SCALI, GIORGIO. Leader of a Florentine faction who in 1382 attacked the palace of one of the magistrates to try to save a friend from punishment. He was beheaded.

SCIPIO. P. Cornelius Scipio Africanus (234–c. 183 BC). Great Roman commander and consul, campaigned successfully in Spain and Africa, where he won a decisive victory over Hannibal. Accused of corruption and retired from Rome.

SEVERUS, L. SEPTIMIUS. Roman emperor AD 193–211. Born AD 146, and held military commands under Marcus Aurelius and Commodus. In 193 was proclaimed emperor by his army in Illyria and marched on Rome. After the death of Julian, he defeated Pescennius Niger, who had been proclaimed emperor by the Eastern legions (194). Two years later defeated Clodius Albinus, who had been proclaimed emperor in Gaul. Died at Eboracum (York).

SFORZA, CARDINAL. Ascanio Sforza. Brother of Ludovico il Moro. Was estranged from pope Alexander VI (whose election he had aided) when Charles VIII was preparing to invade Italy, and joined the Colonna, who were in the pay of France. Subsequently captured by the French after Louis XII took Milan in 1500.

SFORZA (father of Francesco). Muzio Attendolo Sforza (1369–1424). *Condottiere*, trained like his rival, Braccio, under Alberico da Barbiano. Killed in the service of Joanna of Naples.

SFORZA, FRANCESCO (1401–66). Mercenary who entered the service of Filippo Visconti, duke of Milan (1412–47), and married the latter's natural daughter, Bianca Maria. After the death of Visconti he seized the duchy himself (1450). He successfully maintained his position at Milan and five of his descendants were in turn dukes of Milan.

SIXTUS. Pope Sixtus IV, elected in 1471. Francesco della Rovere. His nephew was Giuliano della Rovere, the future pope Julius II. Died 1484.

SODERINI, PIERO. Elected *Gonfaloniere di Justizia* of Florence for life (in effect, head of the state) in 1502. A close friend of Machiavelli. He followed a consistently pro-French policy. Fled from Florence on the return of the Medici in 1512.

THESEUS. Legendary hero of Attica, son of Aegeus, king of Athens. Among other exploits, slew the Minotaur in the Cretan labyrinth.

TITUS QUINTIUS. Flaminius T. Quintius, Roman consul 198 BC. Conducted the war against Philip of Macedon, whom he defeated in 197.

VENAFRO, ANTONIO DA. Adviser and ambassador of Pandolfo Petrucci of Siena whom he helped to become ruler. Was present at Magione, in 1502, when Cesare Borgia's mercenaries formed their conspiracy against him.

VITELLI, NICCOLÒ. Ruler of Città di Castello. Attacked in 1474 by pope Sixtus IV, who built the fortresses which, as Machiavelli says, Niccolò destroyed, after being restored by Lorenzo de' Medici. Died in 1486.

VITELLI, PAULO. Employed as a mercenary by Florence in the operations against Pisa in 1498. Became suspected of treachery, was imprisoned and executed in 1499.

VITELLI, THE. Noble *condottiere* family of Città di Castello in the Roman states.

VITELOZZO. Vitelozzo Vitelli. Mercenary commander, brother of Paulo Vitelli with whom he soldiered in the service of Florence. Escaped when Paulo was executed for treachery. Served Cesare Borgia, took part in the conspiracy against him, and was killed at Sinigaglia in 1502.

XENOPHON. Athenian of the fifth century BC. Accompanied the Greek army which marched under Cyrus against Artaxerxes in 401. Conducted the Greeks on their famous retreat, of which he left a record in the *Anabasis*.

NOTES

Translator's note

1. These Latin chapter headings, along with other internal evidence, have been interpreted as indicating that in much of *The Prince* Machiavelli was motivated by a spirit of contradiction, and that from Chapter XII he was inspired by opposition to earlier Humanist literature on the prince. Cf. Gilbert, *Journal of Modern History*, Vol. XI, No. 4, December 1939.

Letter from Niccolò Machiavelli

1. Lorenzo (1492–1519) was the son of Piero de' Medici and the nephew of Giovanni de' Medici (Leo X), who made him Duke of Urbino in 1516. Giuliano de' Medici, to whom Machiavelli probably intended to dedicate *The Prince* originally, was the brother of Piero and Giovanni (later Pope Leo X), sons of Lorenzo il Magnifico. The Medici princes Lorenzo and Giuliano were used as (idealized) subjects for Michelangelo's powerful sculptures in the Medici chapel of San Lorenzo in Florence.

II. *Hereditary principalities*

1. Machiavelli is conflating two rulers of Ferrara, Ercole I (1431–1505) and Alfonso I (1476–1534).
2. A projection at the end of a wall to provide for its continuation. The word is unusual in English, but so is *addentellato* – Machiavelli's word – in Italian. This passage seems to be the only one in which Machiavelli does use it.

III. *Composite principalities*

1. King Louis XII held Milan from September 1499 to February 1500. Then Ludovico Sforza returned to power only till April 1500, when he was defeated at the battle of Novara. In 1512 the French again lost Milan after their defeat at Ravenna by the army of the Holy League.

2. The Balkan peninsula, subject to Turkish incursions after the fall of Constantinople in 1453.

3. The Romans defeated Philip V of Macedon in 197 BC (at Cynoscephalae) and Antiochus III of Syria in 191 BC (Thermopylae) and in 190 BC (Magnesia).

4. Louis XII of France (1498–1515) held power in Italy from 1499 to 1512. Charles VIII (1483–98) campaigned in Italy from 1494 to 1495, when on his retreat he was defeated at the battle of Fornovo by the allied powers of the Empire, Spain, Venice, Milan, Florence, Naples and Mantua.

5. These 'signori' were Astorre Manfredi, Giovanni di Costanza Sforza, Pandolfo Malatesta, Giulio Cesare da Varana, and Jacopo degli Appiani.

6. In November 1500 in the Treaty of Granada, King Louis and Ferdinand V of Aragon or II of Spain (1452–1516) agreed on the conquest and division of the kingdom of Naples, where Campania and Abruzzi were to fall to France, Apulia and Calabria to Spain.

7. Federigo of Aragon, king of Naples. He surrendered to French forces in 1501.

8. After the formation of the League of Cambrai (1508) Venice was defeated in May 1509 at the battle of Vailà, or Agnadello, and withdrew from the mainland cities.

9. The Romagna was the north-east part of the papal states. The area was never clearly defined.

IV. *Why the kingdom of Darius conquered by Alexander did not rebel*

1. Alexander the Great (356–323 BC) made Macedonia supreme in Greece after the battle of Chaeronea (338 BC) and his succession to Philip II in 336 BC. He first defeated the Persians in 334 BC and eventually invaded India in 327 BC He died in May or June 323 BC, having proved himself a brilliant general and founded scores of cities.

2. A *sandjak* is an administrative district.

3. The civil war between Julius Caesar and Pompey after the former famously crossed the Rubicon in 49 BC.

V. *How cities or principalities which lived under their own laws should be administered after being conquered*

1. In 404 BC after the Peloponnesian war, Sparta imposed oligarchic rule on Athens: the Thirty Tyrants, held power only briefly before 'democratic' rule was restored.

2. Carthage was destroyed by the Romans at the end of the Third Carthaginian War (149–146 BC). Numantia in Spain was destroyed in 133 BC. Capua (north of Naples) was stripped of its privileges as a Roman ally in 211 BC.

3. In the confusion caused by the invasion of Charles VIII in 1494, Pisa (controlled by Florence since 1406) seized its independence and held it till 1509.

VI. *New principalities acquired by one's own arms*

1. Moses, the Hebrew lawgiver, led his people from bondage in Egypt to the verge of Canaan in the thirteenth century BC. Cyrus the Great (d. 529 BC), king of Persia, overthrew Astyages, king of the Medes, *c.* 559–549 BC, following nearly half a century of relative peace. Romulus, according to legend, founded Rome, supposedly in 753 BC, and populated the city with fugitives. Theseus, legendary Greek hero, after many adventures, including killing the Minotaur of Crete, became king of Athens. He defeated the Amazons but was eventually murdered.

2. The Syracusans had been attacked in 270 BC by the Mamertines. Hiero II of Syracuse became king in 269 BC.

3. 'That he had all the attributes of a king except a kingdom.' The quotation is a verbally inaccurate one from the Roman historian Justin.

VII. *New principalities acquired with the help of fortune*

1. Ludovico Sforza (*c.* 1451–1508), called Ludovico il Moro (the Moor), effective ruler of Milan from 1494.

2. Cesare Borgia's first campaign lasted from November 1499 to January 1500. During his second campaign, which started in September 1500, he took Pesaro, Rimini, and Faenza, and threatened Florence itself, before joining the French army marching on Naples. His third campaign saw the capture of Urbino in June 1502 and preparations to attack Bologna in September 1502. Machiavelli had his first audience with Cesare at Imola on 7 October 1502 and followed him to Cesena. Remirro de Orco was murdered on Cesare's orders on 26 December 1502; Oliverotto da Fermo and Vitellozzo Vitelli were strangled during the night of 31 December – 1 January 1503.

3. Antonio Ciocchi da Montesansovino, also called Antonio Del Monte.

4. This was 28 October 1503, after the brief reign of Pope Pius III.

5. Pope Alexander and Cesare were both laid low by fever on 12 August, and the Pope – aged 72 – died on 18 August.

6. These cardinals were respectively: Giuliano della Rovere (Julius II), Giovanni Colonna, Raffaello Riario, Ascanio Sforza.

7. Georges d'Amboise, archbishop of Rouen.

VIII. *Those who come to power by crime*

1. See Glossary of Proper Names. Paulo Vitelli was killed on 1 October 149 '.

2. On 26 December 1501.

IX. *The constitutional principality*

1. Machiavelli contrasts the *grandi* with the *popolo*, the former being loosely the grandees. In ancient Rome, Machiavelli believed, their mutual hostility had been constructive; in Florence it had proved ruinous. Cf. *Istorie Fiorentine* (History of Florence), Book III.

2. The Achaean league of Greeks and Romans, against which Nabis (207–192 BC) fought in alliance with Philip V of Macedon (237–179 BC). Machiavelli's references to Nabis are derived from Livy's *History of Rome* (Book XXXIV).

XI. *Ecclesiastical principalities*

1. Pope Alexander VI.
2. Venice, seeking to expand her land empire, declared war on Ferrara in 1482. A league was formed against her by Sixtus IV, Naples, Milan, and Florence.
3. Cesare Borgia was made Duke of Valence by King Louis XII.

XII. *Military organization and mercenary troops*

1. Machiavelli's phrase is *col gesso*, 'with a piece of chalk'. According to Philippe Comines (*Memoirs VII*), Pope Alexander VI said it.
2. A reference to Savonarola.
3. Filippo Maria Visconti died on 13 August 1447. After the battle of Caravaggio on 15 September 1448, Francesco Sforza, son of Muzio Attendolo Sforza (1369–1424), took control of Milan in 1450. The king of Aragon was Alfonso V, called the Magnanimous.
4. Battle of Vailà, 1509, cf. XXXVI note 4. of *Exhortation to liberate Italy* (see p. 106).

XIII. *Auxiliary, composite, and native troops*

1. At the battle of Ravenna on 11 April 1512, the French defeated the forces of Julius II's Holy League, but their brilliant commander, Gaston de Foix, was killed and soon after, confronted by an army of Swiss, they retreated towards Milan.
2. John VI, Cantacuzenus (*c.* 1292–1383), Byzantine emperor involved in civil war which ended when he took Constantinople in 1347 with Turkish assistance and was reconciled with John V for whom he had been regent.

Civil war broke out again in 1352, and John VI again had Turkish help. He eventually abdicated.

3. The Hundred Years War between England and France ended in 1453 by when a standing army had already been established.

4. In 1512, after the formation of the Holy League and the death of Gaston de Foix, the French retreated into Piedmont from their positions in Italy. On his accession Leo X renewed the Holy League, and France came under military threat from Spain, England, and the Swiss.

5. 'That nothing is so weak or unstable as a reputation for power which is not based on one's own forces.' The Latin is based on a sentence in the *Annals* of Tacitus.

XV. *The things for which men, and especially princes, are praised or blamed*

1. Here as always Machiavelli uses the word *amici* – friends – for those we would call allies.

2. The two words Machiavelli uses are *misero* and *avaro*.

XVI. *Generosity and parsimony*

1. The Italian clause reads: '. . . e nel mondo non e se non vulgo; e li pochi non ci hanno lvogo quando li assai hanno appoggiarsi.' Some Italian texts omit the *non* but I follow Whitfield (*Discourses on Machiavelli* p. 220) in thinking that 'the point is clear enough. . . The generality of mankind do not have the means to act independently, on their own initiative: they lean on authority. If that authority is there, and is strong, then there is no room for the ambition of the few to develop.'

2. Ferdinand II (1452–1516), known as Ferdinand the Catholic, who, with Isabella of Castile, greatly increased the power and possessions of Spain and its monarchy.

XVII. *Cruelty and compassion*

1. Pistoia was a subject-city of Florence, which forcibly restored order there when conflict broke out between two rival factions in 1501–2. Machiavelli was concerned with this business at first hand.
2. 'Harsh necessity, and the newness of my kingdom, force me to do such things and to guard my frontiers everywhere.' *Aeneid* i, 563.
3. Locri Epizephyrii was in Calabria. Machiavelli liked to make comparisons – elaborated in the *Discorsi* – between Hannibal and Publius Cornelius Scipio, called Scipio Africanus Major (236–182 BC), who defeated Hannibal during the Punic wars at Zama in 202 BC.

XVIII. *How princes should honour their word*

1. Ferdinand of Aragon.

XIX. *The need to avoid contempt and hatred*

1. Machiavelli's account of these emperors is based on the history of the Roman Empire from the death of Marcus Aurelius to the accession of Gordian III by Herodian, in whose lifetime many of the events described took place. Machiavelli almost certainly used the Latin translation of Herodian's history (which was written in Greek) published in 1493 by the poet and friend of Lorenzo de' Medici, Poliziano.
2. Machiavelli's Italian is *uno animo ostinato*.
3. The ruler of Turkey in Machiavelli's time was Selim I. By the 'Sultan' he means the ruler of Egypt.

XX. *Whether fortresses and many of the present-day expedients to which princes have recourse are useful or not*

1. Names probably originally derived from the rivalry of the Welf and Weiblingen families for the imperial crown. During the Middle Ages in Italy they came, very loosely, to stand for supporters of the pope (Guelf)

and emperor (Ghibelline). Local and family rivalries confused the issue further, but the Ghibellines tended to be noble and martial, the Guelfs men of industry and commerce.

2. Guidobaldo da Montefeltro was dispossessed effortlessly of the Duchy of Urbino by Cesare Borgia in June 1502, but finally returned after the death of Pope Alexander in 1503. In 1506, after driving Giovanni Bentivogli from Bologna, Pope Julius had a fortress built at Porta Galliera and commissioned a bronze statue of himself from Michelangelo; both were destroyed when the Bentivoglio returned.

XXI. *How a prince must act to win honour*

1. The Italian phrase is *il fondamento dello Stato suo.*
2. Machiavelli is probably referring to the expulsion from Granada of all Moslems over the age of fourteen who did not accept baptism, in 1502. Isabella, rather than Ferdinand, was responsible for this measure. The Moors were finally expelled from Spain in 1610.
3. 'Nothing is more contrary to your interests than their advice, that you should not intervene in the war; you will become the prize of the victor, without favour or dignity.' The passage is based on Livy.
4. The Italian states that a prince must *mostrarsi amatore delle virtù dando recapito alli uomini virtuosi, e onorare gli eccellenti in una arte.*

XXII. *A prince's personal staff*

1. Antonio Giordani da Venafro was a skilled lawyer and persuasive advocate, often mentioned in contemporary political writings.

XXVI. *Exhortation to liberate Italy from the barbarians*

1. Cesare Borgia, almost certainly.
2. Moses, Cyrus and Theseus.
3. 'Because a necessary war is a just war and where there is hope only in arms, those arms are holy.' Again, Machiavelli is quoting Livy.

4. Il Taro – the battle of Fornovo – was fought between the retiring French army and an Italian league in 1495. Alessandria was sacked by the French in 1499, during the first Italian invasion by the army of Louis XII. Capua was taken and sacked by the French in 1501, after the Franco-Spanish attack on Naples. Genoa was taken by the French in 1507 (the pro-French aristocratic party had been overthrown the year before). The Venetians were thoroughly defeated at the battle of Vailà, or Agnadello, by the French in 1509, as part of the operations of the League of Cambray. Bologna was taken by the French in 1511 during the war between them and Julius II. Mestre, near Venice, was burned by the forces of the League between the emperor, Spain, Milan, and the pope in 1513 just before the battle of Vicenza, where the Venetians were defeated.

5. Ravenna was fought in 1512. Cf. Louis XII in the Glossary.

6. This verse translation is that of Edward Dacres, whose excellent version of *The Prince* was first published in 1640. Here is the Italian:

> *Virtù contro a furore*
> *Prenderà l'arme, e fia el combatter corto;*
> *Che l'antico valore*
> *Nell'italici cor non è ancor morto.*